THE COLLECTOR'S HANDBOOK

Tax Planning, Strategy, and Estate Advice from Collectibles Experts for Collectors and Their Heirs

by
James L. Halperin
Gregory J. Rohan

Dallas, Texas

Copyright © 2000, 2004 by James L. Halperin and Gregory J. Rohan

All Rights Reserved.
Reproduction or translation of any part of this work without permission of the copyright owners is unlawful. Written requests for permission or further information should be addressed to:

Ivy Press
3500 Maple Avenue
17th Floor
Dallas, Texas 75219-3941

ISBN: 0-9651041-2-5

Manufactured in the United States of America
2004, Revised Edition

Copyright © Cover Art by Kim Patterson,
Photography by Jody Garver, 2004

"…helpful summaries about care of collections, security, and tax pitfalls." — *The Philadelphia Inquirer*

"Minimize inheritance headaches and heartaches… Experts' tips for winning encounters with coin dealers and the IRS." — *The Centinel*

" Must reading for most of today's collectors." — *Coins Magazine*

"…your heirs deserve knowledge and truth about your holdings. Your use of this book should help, and—especially for those of you with a valuable collection—a copy for your heirs would not be amiss." — *COINage Coin Collector's Yearbook*

"…deserves to be in the hands of any collector of coins, serious or frivolous. It gives excellent advice for maintaining records, caring for, safeguarding and for disposing of a numismatic collection. Dealers would do well to recommend it to their customers—after reading it themselves." — Col. Bill Murray, *Noted Numismatic Columnist*

"…by far the best book written on how to insure that your coin collection is never sold for pennies on the dollar. A book I highly recommend to all my clients." — Dale Williams, *Professional Numismatist*

"A wealth of sound and practical information, written in a clear and concise manner. Must reading for every collector!" — Leroy Van Allen, *Numismatic Author and Morgan Dollar Expert*

"...It is for everyone in numismatics and is even a 'must have' for those who may become heirs, but lack the know-how of what to do next. Senior citizens, like myself, will be especially happy with the interesting stories of estates, etc. ... EVERYONE should own it if coins are involved in their activities. I highly recommend this book..." — *Lee Martin, Founder of the Numismatic Literary Guild*

"How comprehensive is this book? I put it with my collection and told my daughter Sara to read it when it comes to handling my coin estate." — *Fred Weinberg, Past President of the Professional Numismatists Guild*

The first edition of this book, titled *The Rare Coin Estate Book*, received the comments and endorsements listed above, and was also
Winner of the Robert Friedberg Award from the Professional Numismatists Guild:
Best Numismatic Book of the Year

Table of Contents

Acknowledgements vi
Foreword vii

Part 1: Administering Your Collection 1
Chapter 1 – Record Keeping 2
Chapter 2 – Caring for Your Collection 12
Chapter 3 – Safeguarding Your Collection 18

Part 2: Estate Planning for Your Collection 27
Chapter 4 – Include Your Family in Your Plans 28
Chapter 5 – Division of Assets 35
Chapter 6 – Tax Options for Estate Planning 41

Part 3: Evaluating Your Collection 49
Chapter 7 – Third Party Authentication and Grading of Coins ... 50
Chapter 8 – Having Your Collection Appraised 55

Part 4: Disposing of Your Collection 71
Chapter 9 – Selling Your Collection Through Outright Sale 72
Chapter 10 – Selling Your Collectibles Through an Agent 79
Chapter 11 – Selling Your Collection at Auction 86
Chapter 12 – Etiquette & Tips 93

Appendices 105
Appendix A – Numismatic Fraternal Organizations 106
Appendix B – Insurance Companies Offering Collectible
 & Numismatic Coverage 108
Appendix C – Third-Party Grading Services 109
Appendix D – Selected Publications for Collectors 111
Appendix E – HeritageGalleries.com Resources 115

Acknowledgements

In one important aspect, writing a book is like forming a great collection: many people will contribute in many different ways. While collecting, we build on the work of dealers, auction firms, friends old and new, and even those authors whose reference books line our shelves. It is no different when a book is written. We offer many thanks to the following for their assistance during the preparation of this work:

Jody Garver, Cathy Hadd, Mary Hermann, Steve Ivy, Bob Korver, Burnett Marus, Kim Patterson, Matt Pegues, Will Rossman, James Stoutjesdyk, Marsha Taylor, Mark Van Winkle, and Carl Watson.

Foreword

Why We Collect Things

My friend, John Jay Pittman, though not a wealthy man to begin with, built a vast and famous coin collection. He accomplished that feat by studying relentlessly, then shrewdly investing a large percentage of his limited income as a middle manager for Eastman Kodak plus his wife's income as a schoolteacher. In 1954, he mortgaged their house to travel to Egypt and bid on coins at the King Farouk Collection auction. John sacrificed his and his family's lifestyle over the course of many decades. He passed away in 1996, with no apparent regrets, and his long-suffering family justly received the benefit of his efforts when the collection was sold at auction for over $30 million. But why did he do it?

At our website, HeritageGalleries.com, we auction many different types of collectibles in addition to rare coins and currency. Most of our 125,000+ registered client/ bidders collect in more than one area (we know this because we offer a survey on our website, with multiple drawings throughout the year for prizes and free catalogs). Our clients seek many different collectibles, and for many different reasons.

Pittman paid $400 for a Canadian 6-piece 1936 Dot specimen set in 1954; Auctioned in 1999 for $345,000

One fervent collector of historical documents refers to his own collecting propensity as "a genetic defect." More likely, collecting is a basic human instinct; a survival advantage amplified by eons of natural selection. Those of our ancient ancestors who managed to accumulate scarce objects may have been more prone to survive long enough to bear offspring. Even today, wealth correlates to longer life expectancy—and could any form of wealth be more basic than scarce, tangible objects?

But more relevant than the reason you happen to collect Lithuanian first day covers or 1950s romance comic books today, are your long-term goals in seeking them. Understanding your goals may help you achieve them.

If you collect—or ever plan to collect—anything, your first priority should be to develop an honest self-awareness of your personal ambitions. You might even try to predict how those ambitions are likely to evolve throughout the remainder of your life.

For example, in addition to the instinctive predilection previously discussed, the most common reasons people collect things include:

1) Knowledge and learning
2) Relaxation and stress reduction
3) Personal pleasure (including appreciation of beauty, and pride of ownership)
4) Social interaction with fellow collectors and others (i.e. the sharing of pleasure and knowledge)
5) Competitive challenge
6) Recognition by fellow collectors and perhaps even non-collectors
7) Altruism (since many great collections are ultimately donated to museums and learning institutions)
8) The desire to control, possess and bring order to a small (or even a massive) part of the world

9) Nostalgia and/or a connection to history
10) Accumulation and diversification of wealth (which can ultimately provide a measure of security and freedom)

The motives listed above, among others, are not mutually exclusive. The majority of collectors reap several—often most—of these benefits, though some may invest excessive amounts of time, energy, and discretionary funds.

Like John Pittman, Robert Lesser is a true collector, but also a visionary with an ability to change his own course. He funded his subsequent collections by building a fine collection of Disney memorabilia before anyone else was interested, then selling it for a seven-figure sum once the collecting world caught up with him. Lesser went on to assemble, long before anyone else discovered their now-obvious appeal, the all-time greatest collections, of toy robots (museum exhibitions of his collection have attracted sell-out crowds with waiting lines stretching over city blocks) and pulp magazine cover paintings. I *highly* recommend his book on the latter, elegantly titled: Pulp Art.

Robert Lesser's collection of over 250 rare robots and space toys has been exhibited at several museums and is considered among the finest in the world.

Robert Lesser's collection of over 250 rare robots and space toys has been exhibited at several museums and is considered among the finest in the world.

Many non-acquisitive pastimes provide similar levels of satisfaction, knowledge, recognition – and other benefits of collecting. But unlike home gardeners, tropical fish enthusiasts, and similar hobbyists, serious collectors of rare objects will very often find that they have created substantial wealth at the end of the day, especially when they acknowledge, at least to themselves, that doing so is one of their goals.

Whatever your motivations in collecting, this book will help make you a more intelligent collector. Nearly every collection involves making reasonable financial decisions; doing so repeatedly will improve the monetary value you or your heirs ultimately reap from your collecting endeavors, as well as increase your satisfaction. Making your hobby more productive and rewarding is easiest done while you are actively pursuing these pieces of history. We strongly encourage you to follow this advice during your collecting years, so that your heirs aren't left with the struggle of catching up at a time when they are least able.

Jim Halperin

James L. Halperin
Heritage Galleries & Auctioneers
3500 Maple Avenue, 17th Floor
Dallas, TX 75219-3941
Jim@HeritageGalleries.com

PART ONE

Administering Your Collection

CHAPTER one

Record Keeping

"The longest journey begins with a single step — and a record."

Nobody knows your collection as well as you do. The hours you have spent or will spend enjoying it give you a familiarity that another person could never match. As such, no one is more qualified to record your collecting activities than you are. Creating a permanent record for your collection can be either an easy task or a daunting one. While we are sure that the quote below the title of this chapter was created for some other circumstance (likely double-entry book-keeping), there are definite parallels. If you begin an inventory with the first purchase and continue to build it  on a "log as you go" basis, the task will not be onerous, and either you or your heirs (or both) will be rewarded when the journey is done. This is the best solution because the time spent logging each transaction is minimal, the information is fresh, and a pattern of activity is started that will become habit as your collection develops.

Handwritten or Computer Generated – The Choice Is Yours

The important thing is that you create an inventory of your collection. The method you use to accomplish this is a matter of personal preference. Some collectors love numbers and statistics, and may take some additional pleasure in having a well-organized record. This may well take the form of a hand-written ledger, with each item and its history meticulously entered across the columns. Please be honest with yourself, however. If your handwriting is sometimes indecipherable even to you, please consider how difficult (if not impossible) it would be for your heirs to try to understand those illegible entries and guess at your intent. In this rapidly advancing age of computers and software programs, help is available. Many computer software programs have been written to assist in record-keeping of inventories.

If you are somewhat computer literate and either dislike packaged programs or don't want all the "bells and whistles," you can create your own record-keeping file on any spreadsheet program such as Microsoft® EXCEL or WORKS.

Coin Inventory
For coin collectors, HeritageGalleries.com has a free and particularly useful feature called "My Collection" which allows the coin collector to keep a private record of items owned, bought, or sold.

If you use either a manual record or create your own computer file, you need to include at a minimum, the following information:

NECESSARY ITEMS – If creating your own computer file, each of these items should be posted in a separate column to allow easy categorical sorting:

- **Purchase Date**
- **Date** (or approximate date) item was made
- **Mintmark** (if a coin) or other markings (i.e., Publisher – for books)
- **Denomination** (if a coin)
- **Variety** (where applicable)
- **Grade or Condition**
  If you are recording uncertified coins, or un-authenticated collectibles, please consider that your heirs will be inclined to accept your opinion as gospel. If you "stretch," you will both overvalue your collection for estate tax purposes and make it virtually impossible for your heirs to be comfortable with any disposition option.
- **Grading Service or Appraiser** (where applicable)
- **Certificate ID Number** — for coins, comics and cards (where applicable)
  This is the inventory number assigned by the grading service and found on the grading label of the holder. It provides item-specific identification where the collection has multiple identical items and is valuable as a recovery tool in the unfortunate event that the collection was stolen. If you have a software package that does not include this option, you should list this number in the notes field.

- **Purchase Price**
  This information is especially useful for tax purposes, when selling items, and recording capital gains.

OPTIONAL ITEMS might include:

- **Where You Purchased the Item**
  This is a helpful reference for pedigree, recovery issues; particularly valuable if from a recognized auction house and sale. Often, your heirs will not know your major (trusted) sources of collectibles.

- **Related Expenses That Would Impact the Acquisition Cost**
  Acquisition expenses are part of the basis of your collection for estate purposes. If you traveled to an auction or convention to make purchases, reasonable travel expenses relative to the amount purchased may be assigned (more on this later).

- **An Issue Numbering System** (for coins)
  In the case of rare coins, one easy method for sorting and organizing collection records by computer is the use of an issue numbering system that sequences each coin by denomination, date and mint mark. The Professional Coin Grading Service (PCGS) employs such a numbering system. Their numbers are widely recognized in the industry and can be found by acquiring their *Population Report*. An additional benefit in recording purchases using this system is that each PCGS coin has its issue identification number on the grading label.

- **An Inventory Numbering System**
  You might also benefit from having your own inventory numbering system to link the items to the record.

Numbers could be sequential (e.g. 00001), reflect the purchase date (e.g. 9912001), or any other system that makes it easy to pick up a piece of your collection and quickly identify it in the record.

- **Location**
  This is particularly important if your collection is extensive and spread out around your house, in safe-deposit boxes, in different banks, or other storage sites. Also, if you have annotated a group of objects as a single line item on your inventory, try to keep them together in one location.

CONTINUING ITEMS – Once your files are created, two functions are quite important to the process. One is annotating any items that you have sold or traded. (Can you imagine the amount of time your heirs would spend looking for listed objects if you neglected to note that you had sold them ten years prior?) The second is to create a periodic value update. Packaged software may provide this option, but if you're creating your own file, you'll need to consider:

- **Value**
  Value Source. We would recommend that you use a wholesale pricing guide, as something approximating liquidation value is usually more beneficial for estate purposes. You should note the source, so your heirs can use the same one.

- **Last Evaluation Date**
  We recommend that you update your records at least semi-annually and more frequently if you acquire and/or dispose of significant items. Always date the evaluation on the inventory.

- **Sales Date** (if applicable)
  If you sell or trade something, please annotate it in your record. One way of addressing this is to conduct an annual inventory and note either that you found the article or explain its absence. Creating and maintaining the inventory record is paramount, but there are several related tasks that are also important.

- **Retain All Purchase Invoices**
  The IRS loves receipts. Having the majority of your cost basis documented lends credibility to those entries for which no invoice was provided. We recommend that you file your invoices sequentially by purchase date and if you have created your own inventory-numbering system, mark the matching numbers on the invoice.

- **Retain Receipts For Related Expenses**
  Certain expenses surrounding the acquisition, development and disposition of your collection may raise your cost basis, while others may be deductible in the current tax year. Grading service fees, shipping expenses, travel expenses and sales commissions or fees are examples. Rules vary too widely for any simple guideline beyond:

Determining Values

Red Book, Trends, and Coin Dealer Newsletter are popular guides for determining value for coins and currency collectors. The Overstreet Price Guide is used for comics (a digital copy can be obtained from the HeritageComics.com website). Other publications are relevant to each collectible.

keep every receipt and discuss your personal situation with your tax advisor.

- **Maintain Duplicate Records**
  Or back up your computer files. We recommend you keep one inventory at your primary place of residence and one off-site, perhaps in your safe deposit box with your other important papers. This is a safeguard against everything from a computer crash to theft or natural disaster, and is valuable from both an estate planning and insurance claim standpoint.

- **Record Your Wishes in Writing**
  If you wish to leave your collection to a specific heir, or if you wish specific objects to go to different heirs, this *must* be in your will to be effective. New, separate lists should be provided to identify the division of your collection. A very good means of handling it is for you to physically segregate the coins, invoices and other records in accordance with your bequest. Alternatively, the general inventory can be annotated to identify the heir for each line item.

- **Playing "Catch Up"**
  "What if I don't have the records and I've been collecting for many years? How can I recreate them and what is this 'basis' you're talking about?"

Records are extremely important because in their absence, your basis for taxes (which basically means your cost) is the face value in the case of the coins. The task of catching up is ponderous, but necessary, to avoid an unnecessary tax bill. The IRS will generally accept recreated records that attest to the approximate time of purchase with contemporaneous values. The downside is that you will have to acquire the pricing guides for those periods and then maintain copies with your inventory.

In summary, the small steps you take each day in building a record along with your collection will create a valuable legacy. Good records will allow either an orderly disposition in your lifetime or will lessen the burden on your heirs at a time when they would much rather concentrate on honoring your memory. The alternative is discussed below and throughout the book, but it will involve an expensive and time-consuming effort at a most difficult time.

TIPS FOR HEIRS: If you have inherited a collection (or are attempting to evaluate one for probate) and the deceased maintained inadequate records or no records at all, what do you do to protect the interest of everyone concerned?

The first thing any professional will ask is whether you have an inventory list of the collection. It's imperative that you make one.

If the deceased was a *coin collector*, even if there were no records, the coins are probably either in individual holders that identify the issue and (possibly) grade, or in albums that identify the issue. If not and the coins are all loose, you will need to identify the issue. We recommend that you acquire "*A Guidebook of United States Coins*," which should be available at your public library or may be purchased from a local bookstore for around $10.00. Better known as the "R*edbook*" for its cover color, this guide will identify each issue of U.S. coinage, show where the mint marks are located and list significant varieties. The

"*Redbook*" also provides retail values, but as it is published annually, the prices given are often loose estimates.

Arrange your list starting from the smallest denomination and in order of dates within the denomination; then work forward. If the holder shows a grade, include it. If any coins are certified, include the name of the certification service. If you are dealing with sets and partial sets, use your judgment in deciding what to list individually. If the "*Redbook*" indicates little value, you need not write down 75 different dates and mintmarks. For example, the "pennyboard" set of Lincoln Cents beginning in 1940 is worth only a few dollars complete and should be listed as one item. On the other hand, you do need to identify the more valuable coins in a set or partial set. If you have the 1909 – 1939 Lincoln Cents book and it contains only some of the coins, list it as a partial set and mention any issues that the guidebook shows as having a premium (e.g. "A partial Lincoln Cent set 1909 –1939, includes 1909-S, 1914-D, 1924-D and 1931-S").

In the case of comics, take note of the following: If the comic is stored individually in a hard, sealed acrylic package (known as a slab) it will have a grade from one of the comic grading services (generally Comics Guaranty, LLC (CGC) is the most well-known) at the top of the packaging—note whether the grading notes reference any particular pedigree (i.e., Stan Lee Collection, or Gaines File). Also, be sure to record the publication date of each book, and the publication company that printed the book. An Overstreet Price Guide (available online at HeritageComics.com) will help you estimate the value of your collection.

Comic art is a bit more difficult to value appropriately, as with much art, its value is debatable and subject to personal taste. If you can locate the origin of the pieces, you might be able to get a suggested value from the original seller. Note that estimated values for art may differ substantially from dealer to dealer, so auction houses may be the best venue to liquidate a collection. HeritageComics.com is the largest comics and comic art auctioneer in the world. Many questions concerning consignments can be answered on the website.

In the case of other collectibles (Tiffany lamps, antique cuff links, old watches, Colonial American spoons, sports cards and memorabilia) you should also make a list of the items, including as much data as you have available. A knowledgeable dealer may be able to suggest reference books to help you.

When you have completed the list, you are ready for the next step. Appraisals are discussed in depth in their own chapter, but the key point here is that the list you create will assist the professionals you contact in determining the scope of your collection and the type of appraisal that will be most beneficial.

CHAPTER two

Caring For Your Collection

"An ounce of prevention is worth a pound of cure—and a LOT of money!"

State of preservation is one of two main factors influencing the value of a collectible. Unfortunately, if you are unaware of proper storage and handling techniques, an item's state of preservation can diminish while in your care. As a serious collector, you may already have a good

understanding of the process, but it can be more complicated than it appears. Use this chapter as a source for tips, but not as a definitive guide on preservation techniques; the Appendix suggests a few books that give more specific guidance on preserving different types of collectibles (i.e., comics, coins, cards, guns, etc.).

Any valuable collection should be appropriately safeguarded. In the case of many rare items, the condition of an item can raise or lower its value by thousands of dollars, so we would like to impart to you the gravity of maintaining appropriate storage and handling conditions.

Many products routinely sold and used by the collectibles' community are potentially hazardous, and what may be acceptable as a short-term solution can damage your collectibles in the long run. Certainly, you'll want to take the long view, both for your continued collecting enjoyment and for the benefit of your heirs.

Ensure the Proper Storage of Your Collection

You probably view your collection from two perspectives: as items purchased for your personal enjoyment, but necessarily also, as a significant asset that must be protected. No one rule applies for proper collectibles storage, as you will want to weigh the benefit of easy access versus the potential for loss. You will have to make a decision that you find comfortable. The more valuable a collection, the more carefully you may need to protect it from mishandling.

It is important to store your collectibles in holders made of inert plastic materials, those that are composed of little or no chemical substance that might damage your collectible over time. Coin collectors frequently choose Sealed Inert Capsules which prevent outside toxins from reacting with the metallic face and body of the coin. These types of capsules are often included in the cost of coin, comic and sports card grading services. Be sure to inquire about the warranty that the grading service provides.

Because of its rigidity and inert composition, Mylar™ sleeves and holders make particularly good storage devices for flat collectibles. While they may cost more in some cases, they are the only recommended 'long term' storage solution for most paper collectibles, outside of Capsules.

Storage Locations

Physical security will be discussed in the next chapter, but where you keep your collectibles also impacts their state of preservation. Ideally, all collectibles and art should be stored in an environment of consistent moderate temperature and low humidity. A bank safe deposit box fits these criteria, as does an air-conditioned home. These are not, however, always a given.

If you live in Arizona, the humidity is low and you probably have air-conditioning. In Michigan, this may not be the case and you have wild swings in temperature extremes between the seasons. Collectors in South Florida battle high humidity and salt air. It would seem obvious that regardless of where you live, coins should be stored indoors. Nonetheless, we have seen collections stored in garages, outdoor storage units and occasionally buried in the ground. Storing your collection in an environment with a controlled climate is one of the first steps you can take to preserve its value.

Moisture and humidity are culprits that can seriously damage coins. You probably learned early in school what happens when water and metal are in contact for long periods of time. Copper is a particularly reactive metal and is used as an alloy in most United States coins. Corrosion and spotting often result when coins are exposed to moisture or humidity. Bags of silica gel can be used to retard humidity but need to be replaced regularly. The best solution is to simply find a low-humidity environment for your coins, even if it means the inconvenience of a safe-deposit box.

Currency has its own special requirements, but when properly housed, is more durable than one might believe. High humidity should be avoided, but currency should receive some air to maintain its natural fiber. The main culprit for notes is too much direct sunlight, as overexposure will cause the ink to fade and diminish the value. Otherwise, normally cautious packing and storage should be sufficient.

Restoring Your Collection

You should inspect your collection every six months to make sure that it is not being exposed to potential hazards. If you find a problem, or if the information provided in this chapter reveals a potential problem you had been unaware of, how do you correct it? Damage to collectibles is either mechanical or chemical. If the threat is mechanical, simply change the coins to a location or holder that does not present the threat. If the threat is chemical, you first need to determine the immediacy of the danger. As careful as one might be, collectibles do fall victim to these factors, and incur some form of damage.

Ironically, more collectibles have been damaged with good intentions than with bad ones. As such, we mention cleaning options with great trepidation. Unless you are prepared to carefully learn the techniques and practice them with great patience, you would really be better off paying a professional to do the job for you. In either case, no matter how much care is taken, you must also be prepared to accept some cases where the result does not meet your expectations.

The issue of authenticity is again a major factor that should be considered when restoring collectibles. Collectors view restored items as having less integrity than non-restored items. Again, consult an expert before attempting restoration – it is not a process easily reversed.

In summary, caring for your collection is an ongoing process that requires product knowledge, careful planning and routine maintenance. If you've been taking your collection for granted, it's due for an inspection now.

TIPS FOR HEIRS: If you inherited a coin collection, and are not a coin collector, you can do your inheritance more harm than good by almost any attempt to "improve" the collection.

If you did not receive good records and/or guidance in the estate and need to go through the inventory process explained in Chapter 1, the following three rules are basic, yet extremely important:

- Coins should always be held between the thumb and index finger touching only the edge of the coin. Never directly touch the front surface of the coin (known as the obverse) or the back surface (reverse). Natural oils in your skin and/or other contaminants on your fingers leave behind fingerprints that can severely affect a coin's salability and value. Copper and nickel are particularly reactive and susceptible to fingerprints. In short, you should only touch coins the minimum needed to identify the date, mint mark and variety, and it is preferable to accomplish that without touching them at all.
- **DO NOT attempt to clean any of the coins.** The very "dirt" or "tarnish" that is perceived negatively by a non-collector is often prized by the collector for its originality. There are exceptions, but you should consult with a professional to determine what they are. The professional should also give you free advice on storage options and which holders are best for your coins.

- This rule also applies to currency. It's not unusual for older currency to have penciled notations on its surfaces. As some are tempted to clean the "dirty" coin, so are others inclined to erase the offending writing. Please DO NOT attempt to do this. The writing will more than likely NOT come off and the attempt will be both damaging and irrevocable. If you have old currency that was in a box or between the pages of a book, get some Mylar™ holders from a local dealer and store the notes in them. If you have currency in old holders that look "oily," take them to a professional for advice rather than trying to improve them.

If you did receive good records and/or guidance and wish to dispose of the collection, you should deliver the coins or currency to the prospective buyer or auction house "as is" and discuss care issues if the professionals say they have significance. If you are keeping the collection, you may still wish to have a professional examine it to determine if any care problems exist. This is money well spent and it is highly encouraged.

Numismatic Conservation Services is a professional care, cleaning, and conservation firm. They can offer you expert advice if you have "problem" coins. See the appendix for contact information.

CHAPTER three

Safeguarding Your Collection

"Do you want your collection more than the thief does?"

The sad truth is that crimes against property are on the rise. Burglary and simple theft almost qualify as growth businesses. The current arrest and conviction rate is abysmal, and restoration of property even worse. Some of our employees were recently victims of an airport "snatch and grab." The good news was that what the thieves thought were coin cases held only supplies. The bad news was that despite being provided both perpetrator descriptions and a license plate number, the police were not optimistic, or perhaps not interested. The fact that the thieves got the wrong bags made the case relatively "insignificant" in the overall scope of things. We don't know if that kind of attitude is endemic; perhaps there are only enough personnel resources to handle the more serious crimes these days. In any event, it certainly illustrates the need for each of us to upgrade our own attitudes concerning security, particularly if we own the kind of valuables prized by thieves.

Security Versus Access — A Timeless Quandary

Most collectors like to have their collectibles close at hand to study and enjoy at their leisure. That's what collecting is all about. Routinely transporting the collection to and from a safe-deposit box is tiresome at best. Conversely, no one wants to lose his or her favorite collectibles to a burglar. The unfortunate fact is that the inconvenience is constant and the significance of security is apparent only after you've been robbed. As a result, even people who know better may become lax over time. To avoid this, write your own personal security plan and include these elements:

- **Home Security** – your collection is at risk from theft, fire, water damage and other natural disasters. If you are going to keep articles of substantial value at your residence, you should employ several proactive measures to protect them.

  1. Monitored Security System

     A security system is the core of any security plan. This includes both theft and fire alarms that are monitored externally and reported immediately to police and fire departments if triggered. Hardware can be installed for a few hundred to a few thousand dollars and monitoring is only a nominal monthly expense, currently around $25-$75. A monitored security system sends most burglars looking for easier game and puts the more daring ones on the clock. Once the system perimeter is breached, the burglar has only the response time to grab what he can and attempt an escape.

The following devices and practices are designed to minimize the number of valuables a burglar can locate quickly:

2. Home Safe

   Safes are obvious deterrents against theft, but have additional value in the event of fire or natural disaster. Costs are based on size and fire (temperature) "TL" rating. You should make your choice only after discussing your particular needs with an expert. Many insurance companies require a home safe to write a collectibles rider to your Homeowner's Policy, while others will discount the rider based on the quantity and quality of the safeguards you employ.

3. Deterrent Practices

   Whether or not you employ a security system or a safe, there are actions that will reduce the risk of a successful burglary. A primary deterrent is to always leave the impression that someone is at home. This can be accomplished in part by remembering to have your paper and mail held while you are out of town and by putting one or more of your lights on timers. "Beware of Dog" signs (whether or not you own one) on the back fence may ward off a potential burglar.

4. Camouflaging Valuables

   Most people are predictable, and burglars know all the "good" hiding places. They still must deal with external or self-imposed time constraints. The longer a burglar stays in a house, the greater the likelihood of capture; and the burglars know that, too. Things you should know and avoid: most people keep their valuables in the master bedroom followed closely by their home offices if they have one. Guess where burglars go first? So, leave decoys. One gentleman we know has numerous coin albums (filled with pocket change) in plain sight on the bookshelves. Another acquaintance has an old safe that is heavy but moveable. It sits in the corner of his home office and contains absolutely nothing. Its predecessor was taken in a burglary where the thief left several thousand dollars worth of electronic and musical equipment because he thought he'd hit the jackpot. The acquaintance now has a monitored security system and modern (wall) safe, but keeps the decoy as a reminder of the importance of security, and perhaps just a bit of humor about the burglar who only got an empty box (and maybe a hernia). If you don't have a safe, small valuables are best hidden in a false outlet with something plugged into it. A collection of small items should be spread over several non-obvious locations. While you may not be able to totally foil a burglar, you may at least be able to minimize his success.

- **Off-Site Storage & Transport**

    The primary off-site storage option is a safe-deposit box either at a bank or private vault. If you can find a location close to either home or work, the inconvenience factor can be minimized. Sites with weekend access are a major plus, but they are scarce. There's no question that safe-deposit boxes offer very secure storage, but don't let that lull you into complacency. There are still a few storage and security guidelines you need to remember and follow.

    1. Rent a box that's big enough to hold everything easily.

2. Use a desiccant such as silica gel to remove any moisture, and change it regularly.
3. Never forget that your greatest security danger is in transporting the collectibles to and from the box. Use a nondescript bag or carry-all to hold them, and try not to carry too much weight at one time.
4. Have someone drive you to the box site or park as close to the entrance as possible to minimize your time on the street with the valuables.
5. Avoid establishing a pattern in picking up or dropping off your collection.
6. Be aware of what's happening around you when transporting your collectibles. Check your rearview mirror frequently. If you think a vehicle may be following you, do not drive directly to your home. Make several detours that do not follow any logical traffic pattern and see if you lose the suspect vehicle. Know where the closest police station is and if you become firmly convinced that you are being followed, drive directly there.
7. Carry a cell phone with you when transporting valuables. A frightening new robbery technique is to rear-end a vehicle and then rob the victim when he or she gets out to assess the damage and exchange insurance information. You'll have to use your judgment for the situation, but if you're carrying valuables and get rear-ended, you should stay in the car and call 911 on the cell phone. Don't hesitate to tell the operator that you're carrying valuables and are concerned about the possibility of robbery. If you really believe that it's a setup, don't stop; call 911 and tell them your intent while driving to the police station.

8. Airports have also become a favorite work place for thieves. There's a steady flow of people, noise, confusion and a sense of urgency from trying to meet deadlines in an unfamiliar environment. The usual method is the snatch and grab; the thief targets someone who appears distracted, grabs their briefcase or bag and melts into the crowd. A variation is to work in teams where baggage is being unloaded at the curb. One or more of the thieves will distract the victim, while others will grab the bags and then all will make their escape in a waiting vehicle. Your only protection is constant vigilance. You should always have either a grip or your foot on any case containing valuables and should become doubly suspicious if a stranger tries to engage you in conversation. Strange as it sounds, some people carry a loud whistle when transporting valuables. If someone attempts to grab a bag and you start blowing the whistle, the thief is put on the defensive. Everyone else in the area stops to see what the noise is all about so the thief loses the camouflage of the crowd.

- **Shipping**

    Occasionally, you may need to ship valuable articles to another party, and again, there are rules to follow that will minimize the possibility of loss. First and foremost, do not put anything on the outside of the package that would hint at its contents. If an address contains identifying words—coins, numismatics, gold, antiques, or anything similar—use initials instead. Additionally, look at the container you're using. We recently received a package from another dealer whose mailing address labels used initials, but the shipping person packed the coins in a *"Redbook"* box that was clearly marked, *"Guidebook of U.S. Coins."*

Pack the items securely so that they do not rattle and betray their presence. Loose spaces (such as in tubes) should be filled. Pieces of Styrofoam "peanuts" are good for this purpose. Make sure that your shipping box is strong enough for the included weight and bind it with strapping tape. If you are using Registered Mail (the preferred method for most collectors), the post office has a requirement that all access seams be sealed with an approved paper tape.

Method of shipment is a choice that weighs value, risk and cost. USPS 1st Class or Priority Mail with Insurance is the most cost-effective method up to $500 value. The rate of loss has dropped considerably over the last decade, so this is a reasonable option for inexpensive items that can be replaced. Above $500 value, Registered Mail with Postal Insurance is both cost-effective and extremely safe. The one caveat is that the real insurance maximum for registered mail is $25,000. The Post Office wants you to indicate if the contents exceed that amount, and will charge you more for a higher claimed value; they will not, however, pay more than $25,000 on a claim. If you have more value than that, you will need to send multiple packages or seek supplemental private insurance. FEDEX, UPS and other private shippers have become popular in recent years. They offer fast, guaranteed delivery with a high success rate. They also appear to offer some insurance options, but rare coins are specifically excluded. You will need to get private insurance coverage if you wish to use one of these shippers, or you may ask the other party if they have a shipper account and insurance that would cover the shipment.

- **Insurance**

    No matter how many security measures you employ to protect your collection, you also need to acquire suitable insurance to protect you should you suffer a loss of part or all of the collection. This can also be a complicated area as insurance companies write policies in a language all their own. We're not trying to criticize insurance companies; they're in business to make money and they perform a valuable service. As someone seeking protection, though, you need to understand that contract language will generally favor the insurance company, and you need to know exactly what you're getting. That means asking questions. In the case of coins, you need to be particularly certain of what coverages apply when the coins are at home, in a safe-deposit box or in transit, as well as any additional security requirements for each circumstance. It is not a cut-and-dry situation. For example:

    Most Home Owner's policies DO NOT insure your coin or jewelry collection beyond $1,000 (combined with all other items defined as a "valuable"). Your insurance company can usually offer you a rider for more specific coverage, but as it's not their standard business, they are typically not very flexible. You would have to provide a fixed inventory and it would likely be a major paperwork exercise to change it when you buy or sell.

    Some insurance companies may require an "appraisal for insurance." If you choose a company that has this requirement, guidance is available in Chapter 8.

Like most business circumstances, you should analyze your options against your personal situation and then shop for the best deal. In this specialized field, the best option often comes from a company that is familiar with the needs of collectors. If this route appeals to you, we have listed several companies in the Appendix titled, "Insurance Companies Offering Collectible and Numismatic Coverage." In the case of collectibles other than coins, you may want to ask a dealer to recommend a knowledgeable insurance company.

Coins and other small items are popular with burglars and thieves. Regretfully, the risk involved means you need to temper your enjoyment of collecting with some caution. In addition to the measures already suggested, you need to be careful about discussing your collection (and where you keep it) with others. It's said that any piece of information shared with one person reaches ten, and an interesting piece of information—well, use your imagination. Enjoy your collection, but stay vigilant.

TIPS FOR HEIRS: This chapter contains advice that may be the most important you will read. Seasoned collectors are generally very security conscious, but those who only recently have come into possession of a collection must immediately understand the risks and responsibilities that come with this unfamiliar asset. Most importantly, get the collection (if it's small enough) to a safe deposit box immediately. Until you have it safely tucked into a bank vault, don't tell anyone about it. With larger objects, you may want to consult with an insurance agent about the best way to safeguard them until they can be dispersed.

PART two

Estate Planning For Your Collection

CHAPTER four

Include Your Family in Your Plans

"Planning for your eventual passing will always be unpleasant, but the best time to start planning for it is today."

We seriously doubt any adult in America has not read or heard of the importance of making a will, and yet every year, tens of thousands of Americans who would have benefited from wills die intestate (without a will). The reason is simple: nobody likes to think about death, much less actively prepare for it. It may be even worse for collectors. As much as people hate to contemplate their own demise, collectors are equally loath to consider the sale of their collectibles. Perhaps they equate the two events.

Since you're reading this book, we hope that you are at least willing to think about the ultimate disposition of your acquisitions. Whether you intend to collect to the end, or sell next month, much of the same advice applies. We have helped thousands of people dispose of their collections, and more than 20% were heirs who knew next to nothing about the collectibles. That is a statistic that we would like to change. You should too.

Involve Your Family

Many collectors keep their families in the dark about the scale and nature of their collecting. We understand that the reasons for this may be myriad and viewed strictly in the present sense, they may very well suit your situation and preference. Taking a longer view, however, have you considered what effect an untimely demise might have on your collection? What would your heirs' expectations be? We have seen both extremes.

One call from Widow Smith brought us to a house where we found a dining room table covered with boxes of world coins to a height of three feet. From a distance, it was one of the most impressive collections that we had ever inspected: all matching coin boxes, all neatly labeled with the countries of origin. The widow told us that her husband had been a serious collector for more than three decades, visiting his local coin shop nearly every Saturday. He then came home and meticulously prepared his purchases, spending hour upon happy hour at the table in his little study. We opened the first box, and couldn't help but notice the neat and orderly presentation: cardboard 2x2s, neatly stapled, crisp printing of country name, year of issue, Yeoman number, date purchased, and amount paid. We also couldn't help but notice that 90% of the coins had been purchased for less than 50 cents, and the balance for less than one dollar. The collection was box after box of post-1940 minors, all impeccably presented. All essentially worthless.

We asked the widow Smith if she had any idea of the value of the collection. She replied that she knew that rare coins were valuable, and since her late husband had worked so diligently on his collection for so many years, she hoped it would enable her to afford a nice retirement in Florida. It was obviously a very delicate moment. We had to carefully explain that we were neither interested in the coins for auction, nor for direct purchase. Her husband had enjoyed himself thoroughly for all those years, but he had never told her that he was spending more on holders, staples and boxes than he was on the coins. Her dreams of comfortable retirement dashed, we put her in touch with two dealers who routinely purchase such coins. (She refused to consider an offer from the local dealer who had sold most of these coins to her husband.) Mr. Smith's fault was not in his collecting, for his love of these coins was manifest, but in his failure to let his wife know exactly what he was doing.

We more typically encounter widows and heirs on the other extreme. When your spouse spends $50,000 or $100,000 on rare coins or other collectibles, you generally have some knowledge of those purchases, but not always, and not always to the full extent of the purchases. Rare collectibles at this level are definitely an asset that needs to be given appropriate consideration. Unfortunately, however, because they are a hard asset, and one that easily falls outside of prying eyes, some heirs make their distributions without first gathering all of the facts.

Miss Jones was the younger of two sisters who were dividing their father's estate. Dad had left Germany in the early 1930s. As historians will note, this was not particularly a great time to immigrate to America, although it was certainly an excellent time to be leaving Germany. Dad brought to America two collections: antique silver service pieces and his rare coins. The coins were mostly sold to establish his mercantile concern in Iowa. He prospered despite the hard times, and he spent the next thirty years rebuilding his collection of Germanic/European coinage. At the same time, he kept expanding his collection of silverware lovingly created by 17th & 18th century German silversmiths. We knew every aspect of his collecting history, because he had left a meticulous record on index cards. Every coin, every piece of silver was detailed with his cataloging and purchase history. Even his own daughter was moved to compliment his passion for keeping such detailed records.

After his death, his daughters decided to split his collections between themselves. They added up the purchase values of each of his collections. We do not think it was coincidental that the two collections came out just about equal. The older sister/executor had some small knowledge of antique silver, and since she wished to keep all of the elegant heirloom tea service for herself, she decided to keep the silver and give her younger sister the coins. She was definitely not interested in splitting the heirlooms. She sold the non-family silver pieces through a regional auction house, and bragged of realizing more than $200,000 from her father's $27,000 investment.

The younger sister came to us with just one box of his coins. Her father's records for that box indicated a cost less than $2,000, but knowing the years when he had collected, we were anticipating at least a few nice coins. We were, however, totally unprepared for the numismatic feast which was laid before us: pristine coins of the greatest rarity—wonderful, gorgeous coins, most of which had been off the market for at least twenty years. His "$2,000" box was worth more than $150,000, surpassing her wildest expectations.

Miss Jones then produced the record cards for the rest of the collection, and we offered to travel back to Iowa with her the same day. When we finished auctioning the coins, she had realized more than $1.2 million.

One more example of what can happen when information is not shared, and we warn you, the ending is a bit of a shocker. The wife of a deceased coin dealer once called us to consign one million dollars in rare coins from her late husband's estate. Since her self-employed husband had been ill for some time, this asset represented a significant portion of her entire retirement funding. We eagerly picked up the coins, and had already begun cataloging and photographing when we received an urgent phone call from her attorney. The coins had to be returned immediately. It seems that her husband had been holding the extensive coin purchases of his main customer in his vaults, and he had neither informed his wife nor adequately marked the boxes. Most of her $1 million retirement asset belonged to someone else. Failure to adequately inform heirs doesn't happen just to collectors.

A final example, one that really distressed us, demonstrates that partial planning, no matter how well intentioned, can't always guarantee the desired results. A collector with a sizeable collection divided his coins equally (by value) between his adult son and daughter, with instructions that they should seek expert advice before selling. The daughter came to us, and we were pleased to report that her father had done an excellent job of dividing the collection – as expertly as we could have advised. The daughter's coins were worth in excess of $85,000. After she signed the Consignment Agreement, she told us the rest of the story. Her brother had "sold" his share eight months earlier to a local pawnbroker for less than $7,500. Her father hadn't shared his knowledge of the asset's value with his children for fear that his son would spend the money foolishly. Instead, her brother basically gave it away.

So, what should you do to prevent such problems?

Get Your Family Involved — One Way or Another

One of the greatest joys of collecting involves not just the objects of interest, but the friends we make along the way. If passing your collection to the next generation is desirable, you will want to organize an orderly transition. If they just aren't interested in sharing your love of the collectibles, you will have to decide whether to dispose of the collection in your lifetime, or pass that task to your heirs. If the latter, your family should – at a minimum – have a basic understanding of your collection, its approximate value, and how you want it dispersed.

Important Questions to Be Discussed

- **Are there heirs who will want the collection from a collector's standpoint?**
- **Where are the objects kept?**
- **Where is the inventory of the collectibles kept?**
- **What is the approximate value of the collection?**
- **Do any of the articles in your possession belong to someone else?**

- Is there a dealer or other expert that you trust to provide guidance to your heirs?
- Is there a firm that you and your heirs will wish to use to aid in the collection's disposition after your death?

In summary, talk with your family about your collection. The horror stories beginning this chapter are all true and they won't be the last. If, for whatever reason, you cannot bring yourself to share this information with your whole family, pick one trusted individual— perhaps the person you are considering to be your Executor. If even that won't work for you, please take the time to write detailed instructions, or simply make notes in this book, and leave it in your safe-deposit box or wherever you keep your valuables. The next few chapters will further define your options and finding help to implement them. Whatever your choices, the written instructions can be either part of your will or, at the very least, a document kept with the collection inventory. Your heirs will thank you for this final attention to detail.

TIPS FOR HEIRS: This chapter doesn't address inheritance issues, but communications can be initiated from any direction. Do you have a parent with a collection? Certainly it is an issue that requires tact, but such a discussion may save considerable heartache and misfortune later. Additionally, if you know in advance that your spouse or relative has named you as Executor in a will, a few conversations about the collection will make your job much easier.

CHAPTER five

Division of Assets

"No single event has greater potential for dividing a family than dividing an inheritance."

Inheritances bring out the best in some people and the worst in others. It's a sad fact that within even the most stable families, some members will view their relative worth only in tangible terms. In the highly charged emotional environment surrounding the loss of a loved one, any weaknesses in the relationships of those left behind are magnified. Suspicious minds are a bit more finely honed and if the estate is left to the  survivors to divide, it doesn't take much of a spark to ignite a small conflagration. You can minimize the likelihood of a family meltdown by seeking sound legal advice in preparing your will and by leaving precise, written instructions dividing your assets among your heirs.

Instructions in regard to collections are particularly important because they generally involve a large number of pieces with valuations that are not obvious based on appearance alone. This can lead to conflict.

The simplest option (administratively) is to leave the collection intact to one heir. You should have the collection appraised (see Chapter 8 titled "Having Your Collection Appraised") and may, at your discretion, use that basis for dividing the balance of your estate. If your estate contains more than one collection (and an equal or structured division is part of your plan) you should have the other collections appraised as well to determine parity. Your attorney can provide the appropriate verbiage for your will. This is stated as the simplest option because there will be no question as to the physical division of the collection after your death.

If you divide one collection among your heirs, the paperwork burden increases. You must then detail what individual pieces go to whom, expand the scope of the appraisal, and more precisely define the locations of each recipient's portion. Alternatively, you may decree "equal shares." This will also require a detailed appraisal, but may create problems if two heirs want the same items, or if some heirs want to keep certain articles and others want to sell. You should objectively consider your family dynamics in making this decision.

We frequently hear the lament that nobody else in the family cares about collectibles. Perhaps it's because so many individuals get serious with their collecting after their kids are grown. We know how difficult it can be to budget for collectibles when there are dentist bills, clothing, food and tuition bills to pay. By the time the kids are grown, most of them have developed their own hobbies and interests. Be that as it may, we doubt that you would want your family to suffer financially over their choice of leisure activities. *A simpler alternative here is to make a will directing that the articles be sold, with the proceeds shared equally instead of the cumbersome process of dividing a collection equally.*

The question arises whether the collection should be disposed of in your lifetime. From our experience with thousands of these situations, we can affirm that it is easier to divide the proceeds of a sale than the collectibles themselves. The reasons are quite logical. Members of your family may vicariously appreciate the pleasure that your collection brought to you, but unless they are collectors themselves, they are unlikely to keep your collectibles. If you can accept that, ask yourself whether they would handle the disposition as carefully and knowledgeably as you would? If this represents a significant asset to them, are they prepared to manage it properly?

We can understand if you are simply unable to part with your treasures, particularly if working with your collection is a major activity and source of enjoyment in your life at present. If this is the case, we strongly recommend that you prepare a *written disposition plan* for your heirs and keep it with your inventory. Whether you intend to collect for three years, seven or a lifetime, you need to prepare now as if you will not be available to provide guidance later. These are hard words, but we doubt that any person wants to see the family suffer a financial loss through the combination of poor planning and an untimely demise or incapacitation.

The upside of choosing disposition in your lifetime is that you retain control of the process and possibly garner some recognition of your collecting accomplishments.

You also minimize the possibility of an uninformed disposition after your death. You might think that since it's harder to spend collectibles than cash, that such a gift will prevent unwise behavior, but the pawnshop story mentioned previously is just one of many that we've heard.

Another option that bears mentioning is the *gift of your collection to charity*. Some collectors have substantial capital gains in their collections and a charitable gift makes a great deal of sense for their particular situations. If you entertain such thoughts, we must also point out that most charities know virtually nothing about collectibles or disposing of such assets. If you wish for your donation to make a meaningful contribution, you will want to ensure that the charity receives the top dollar from your collection. In this case, unless you are donating the collection to a museum that will display it, it is probably better to sell it in your lifetime while you can see the good works that the donation can create. You should talk with the charity and your lawyer or tax adviser to determine what specific option(s) would best suit your individual situation.

If you simply cannot bear the idea of selling your collection, then you must leave detailed instructions for the disposition of your gift. Most charities will have little real knowledge, and even less affection for your collection than a family heir. They would much rather spend their efforts putting your cash to good use than converting your collection to cash. (Conversely, we just sold a $50,000+ rarity for a Michigan charitable institution that was donated as a "common" coin. In all situations, professional knowledge is the key.) We recommend that your collection be sold via auction, by an auctioneer who is knowledgeable about your collectibles—with the charity of your choice named as beneficiary. This solution ensures that you can keep your collection for your lifetime, that the collection will receive knowledgeable treatment in its disposition, and that your charity will receive the maximum return without expending its personnel resources. You can also recommend or designate a specific auctioneer to handle the disposition.

In summary, your collection is yours to enjoy now and yours to dispose of as you see fit. The 'old saw' says, "You can't take it with you." You can, however, ensure that either the collection or its proceeds provide as much positive influence for others as it has for you.

- Make an action plan for your collection, even if you anticipate many more decades of collecting. You can always update it as you go; you cannot, however, start one after you're gone.

- Read the remaining chapters in this book for options.

- Talk with your advisors and determine which recipient(s), timing and method of disposition make the most sense for you.

- If the timing is now, select the agent appropriate to the method and proceed accordingly.

- If the timing is later, prepare detailed written instructions and leave copies with both your collection and your will. If you prefer your collectibles to be distributed among family members, leave specific instructions as to how that distribution is to be accomplished. If you prefer to distribute the proceeds, make sure you leave directions for non-experts to follow in contacting a firm that is trustworthy. Your instructions should be as detailed as necessary to accomplish your wishes.

TIPS FOR HEIRS: This is another chapter which can aid you only if someone else reads and heeds it. You can, however, point it out to your loved one and discuss it with them whenever it seems appropriate. Good communication between family members often helps everyone avoid the pitfalls of estate planning and transfer. Maybe getting involved in Dad's collecting activities will create a new and lasting bond. You may even come to enjoy collecting yourself.

CHAPTER **six**

Tax Options For Estate Planning

"Taxes are usually underpaid out of intent, but overpaid out of ignorance."

Once again, the United States tax code has run amok. Much as casino gambling rules are written to favor the house, so is the tax code written to favor the government. The core advantage is that the government's representatives can claim you owe virtually anything, and the burden of proving otherwise is on you. Throw in the continuing annual "improvements," Congressionally mandated exceptions, exemptions and "simplifications," and the result is well beyond the understanding of most if not all Americans. Indeed, even IRS employees manning the Tax Help Hotline give incorrect advice roughly 20% of the time.

It is both ironic and symptomatic that the IRS does not accept financial responsibility for those errors. Similarly, while the IRS may recalculate a mathematical error in your favor, they will not point out legitimate deductions that would have reduced your tax bill. Nor will they advise you on how both your financial holdings and estate can be legally structured and positioned to minimize the tax bites of capital gains and estate taxes. That is your responsibility and right or wrong, it is a reality you need to face. If your holdings are substantial, it is well worth the expense of engaging experts to lead you through the fiscal minefield.

This chapter deals with some of the options available for estates with collections. Depending on your personal circumstances, the decisions you make may impact the amount of ordinary income, capital gains, gift and/or estate taxes that you or your heirs have to pay. This chapter is provided solely to improve your general understanding, for we cannot know or advise how any of the options would apply to your personal situation or holdings. We strongly recommend that after studying this information, you engage the services of a competent legal professional, preferably an attorney who is board-certified in Real Estate, Trusts and Probate by your state, or a tax advisor, preferably a CPA who specializes in taxes. Feel free to ask as many questions as it takes to address your interests and concerns, and between the two of you, you should be able to create the plan that best fits your needs and wishes.

Most of the tax-saving options can be accomplished only during your lifetime. If you have ceased actively collecting, there are definite advantages to early disposition. If not, there are also some compromise positions that can allow you to enjoy some control of the collection and some tax benefits as well.

Is Your Collection Worth More Today Than When You Purchased It?

Many collections appreciate over time, but there are exceptions. If you were unfortunate enough to have been the victim of an unscrupulous seller, a current appraisal may show you to be in a loss position. If so and disposition is your intention, you may sell the collection by any method and use the loss to offset an equal amount of capital gains, and you may currently deduct up to $3,000 of excess capital loss annually as well. If, more typically, the collection has appreciated, many other issues come into play.

Give Portions of Your Collection to Your Heirs Now

Estate taxes can be punitive. There is an exemption as of 1999 of $650,000 with indexed increases into the future, but tax rates on the balance of your estate could be as much as 55%. You can reduce your taxable estate through gifts to your heirs during your lifetime: $10,000 annually (per recipient) is permissible without incurring gift taxes. The gift could be appraised portions of your collection or other assets. Recipients must be relatives, but the guidelines are quite liberal. Your advisor will be able to tell you how far the allowance extends.

Donate Your Collection to a Public Charity

If your collection has appreciated, you may be able to enjoy some fiscal benefit while avoiding the trauma of seeing it broken up and sold, through a charitable donation to a public charity. For example, say the cost of your collection was $10,000, but the current fair market value is $60,000. You donate the collection to a qualifying charity.

If you are in the 39.6% tax bracket, your tax savings are $23,760— still a great improvement on your basis with all the positive intangibles of charitable giving. Here's what it takes to qualify:
- The collection is qualified capital gain property. This means essentially that everything included has been in the collection for at least a year, was not created by you, nor was it a gift from the creator. The last portions of those qualifications are based on art law, but if you have medallic art (i.e., medals or tokens)or other privately issued exonumia (items related to coin production) in your collection, they might apply.
- The donee organization is a qualified public charity. Public charities generally receive at least part of their support from the public. Examples might be churches, schools, museums and so on. Private foundations, on the other hand, do not qualify for the deduction of fair market value for your collection. You would need verification from the intended donee on its exemption ruling under both section 501(C)(3) and section 509(A). Typically, you will receive a deduction of only your cost for a donation to a private charity versus full fair market value for a donation made to a public charity.
- The donee organization must be able to make "related use" of your donation. Your gift of tangible personal property must relate to the donee organization's mission or purpose that resulted in their section 501 exemption. For example, you could donate a coin collection to the ANA or ANS to expand their museum collections and receive a deduction of fair market value. Obviously, a coin collection would relate to missions of increasing the knowledge and enjoyment of coin collecting. You

could not donate such a collection to a hospital and deduct the fair market value. The deduction would be reduced by 100% of the appreciation above your cost.

- The collection has a "qualified appraisal" – Essentially, a qualified appraisal is one that is performed by a "qualified appraiser." That is an individual who holds himself out to the public as an appraiser and who is expert in the particular type of property being evaluated; is cognizant of the civil penalties possible for a fraudulent overstatement of value; and is totally independent of the property and parties to the donation. There is a checklist of information required; your advisor and appraiser will be familiar with this.

Your advisor will also counsel you on allowable percentages of your contribution base, section 68 limitations, and possible Alternative Minimum Tax consequences.

Donate a Fractional Interest in Your Collection to a Public Charity

Don't want to give up your collection interests, but still want some tax relief now? You might consider donating an undivided fractional interest in your collection to a qualified charity. Let's say, for example, that you donate one half interest in the collection to a qualifying museum. Each of you gets to keep the collection for six months of each year and you get to deduct half the fair market value of the collection in the year of the donation. This would be ideal if you collect during the cooler months, but gravitate toward the outdoors in summertime. This is also a good technique of charitable contribution when your contribution base (adjusted gross income) is not large enough to support the entire donation because of percentage limitations.

Some donors structure their contribution to give, say 25% of their collection now, 25% in five years, a third 25% in ten years and the remainder at their death. Any percentage of the collection not donated will become part of your estate. If you perceive the possibility of friction between the charity and your heirs over the remaining divided interest, you may wish to complete the donation as part of your will. This method also allows the value of the collection to continue appreciating, so each subsequent donation may be for a greater amount than the previous ones. Interim appraisals would, of course, be necessary.

Charitable Remainder Trusts

A charitable remainder trust is of great value if you are in need of both income and a tax deduction, and are prepared to give up your collection now. It is particularly advantageous if the collection has enjoyed significant appreciation since purchase. In this arrangement, the donation is made to the qualifying charity in trust. The charity agrees to pay you annually either a fixed amount of money (annuity trust) or a percentage of the trust's total value (unitrust) for life or for a set number of years (not to exceed 20).

The benefit is that if you sold the collection yourself to create income, the principal amount would be reduced by taxes on the capital gains. The trustee can sell the collection tax-free and create a larger principal base. You can also claim the collection's cost as a charitable deduction in the year that the trust is initiated (you cannot claim "fair market value" because the sale disqualifies the greater deduction under the "related use" clause). You receive your agreed-upon payments and when the trust period is complete, all remaining interest in the trust passes to the charity.

There are some caveats. Most collectibles (including coins) are not "income producing assets," so the collection (or at least most of it) may have to be sold in the first year of the trust to fund it with qualifying financial vehicles. The annual distribution to the donor must be a minimum of 5% of the trust's value and a maximum of 50%. Additionally, at the conclusion of the agreement, the remainder to the charity must be at least 10% of the initial value. These rules are subject to change, and create a certain amount of latitude in the trust agreement that must be negotiated between the donor and the charity. Again, we strongly recommend that you use the services of a competent attorney or tax advisor to represent you.

In summary, there are many options available to you, each with specific benefits and pitfalls. We have stated this several times previously, but we cannot reiterate enough: **engage a professional to assist you**.

If you are the surviving spouse of the deceased, exemptions generally allow the estate to pass without tax. The estate planning burden then becomes yours, however, as the same exemptions will not apply at your death unless you remarry. If this eventuality was not already considered in your planning, you should contact an estate or tax professional without delay. Even if the survivor's position was considered in the original planning, it cannot hurt to re-evaluate the situation with your attorney.

TIPS FOR HEIRS: As an heir to a taxable estate, most of your opportunities for tax abatement are past. If you are privy to the will of your parent (or other person to whom you will be an heir), perhaps you can advise the person to seek counsel if it is obvious from what you've read that the need exists. After the fact, you can exercise only a little damage control. If it is necessary to liquidate all or part of the collection to pay estate taxes, the expenses of that liquidation (shipping, auction fees, commissions, etc.) should be deductible from the estate. It is often much simpler to buy a paid-up life insurance policy to cover the tax. Again, a tax professional is well worth consulting.

PART three

Evaluating Your Collection

CHAPTER seven

Third Party Authentication and Grading of Coins

Authenticity and evaluation are vital matters for any collection; this chapter deals with having a third-party grading service authenticate your collectibles. These services are most widely available for coins, sports cards and comics. Use them as needed, but it is important to consider the cost, quality and value of grading services for your collectibles. For many items, especially lesser-valued pieces, grading is probably unnecessary.

For coin grading, the American Numismatic Association (ANA) adopted Sheldon's 70-point grading system and, between 1973 and 1977, worked to establish standards for all series under the leadership of numismatic luminary Abe Kosoff. Experts from all coin specialties collaborated with Mr. Kosoff, and the first official ANA grading guide was published in the 1977-1978 time frame. Initially, it recognized three grades to evaluate Mint State coins: Uncirculated or MS-60; Choice Uncirculated or MS-65; and Perfect Uncirculated or MS-70. Unfortunately, the third grade (MS-70) was mostly theoretical, and the two remaining designations quickly proved inadequate for the marketplace. MS-63 (Select Uncirculated) and MS-67 (Gem Uncirculated) were added and worked for awhile before the demand for closer evaluation required even more grades. Eventually, all numbers between MS-60 and MS-70 were employed and the adjectival equivalents often dropped.

NGC and PCGS remain the acknowledged leaders for coin grading. The secret of their success is that to date, they alone have maintained sufficient dealer confidence to be traded routinely on a sight-unseen basis. As such, while we will list the contact information for several grading services in the Appendix, we will address only NGC and PCGS in the text.

Comics and cards are generally graded on a ten-point scale, with a '10' being the most perfect quality for that particular item. Several grading services are listed with their contact information for each of these collectible genres in the Appendix. For comics, Comics Guaranty, LLC (CGC) is recognized as the most trusted grading service. Heritage Comics (HeritageComics.com) offers a discount off of standard CGC grading costs, and more information can be obtained from the company website.

Sports card authenticity is often trusted to one of three major grading houses: Professional Sports Authenticator (PSA), Beckett Grading Services (BGS) and Sportscard Guaranty LLC (SGC). Talk with your local card dealers about which grading service they give the most credibility to. Collectors of Sports and Celebrity autographed items use PSA/DNA to authenticate their collectibles. Again, their website (see Appendix) is the best place to find submission instructions.

Stamp collectors frequently rely on the grading services of Professional Stamp Experts (PSE). The PSE website (see Appendix) contains detailed instructions and an online submission kit which are good guides on how to safely submit stamps for grading.

What Should You Certify?

Certification is an expensive proposition that should not be approached hastily. At $15-$85 an item, the total bill for even a small collection can easily run into the thousands of dollars. Few people are prepared to make that kind of commitment. Naturally not all collectibles benefit equally from being certified. The rule of thumb, of course, is that the finished product has to be worth more than the raw (ungraded) item plus the certification fee. But just what does that mean?

There are two practical reasons to certify a collectible: determine authenticity and to add value. When a dealer considers buying an uncertified collectible, he is trying to guess how the grading service is going to grade it, always giving himself the benefit of the doubt in case of error. For example, if a dealer is looking at your 1886-O Morgan dollar and he is trying to decide whether NGC is going to grade it an MS-63 (valued at $1,780) or MS-64 (valued at $5,300), he is going to figure it as an MS-63 coin to be on the safe side, and offer a price commensurate with an MS-63 coin. This is only fair, as the alternative would leave him with both the risk and the expense, and that is not a formula that works in business. You, however, could have the coin certified before attempting to sell it. Your upside is that if the grading service calls it an MS-64, you have a $5,300 coin. The downside is the cost of the grading fee. The bottom line is that this issue has a significant value spread between grades and (in our opinion) the risk is worth the expense.

Submitting Your Coins

NGC and PCGS both operate primarily through authorized dealer networks. Most of these dealers will gladly submit your coins to their respective grading services on your behalf. The dealer is often compensated with a rebate of approximately 20% of the grading fee. Don't ask him for part of the rebate, but do ask him to preview the coins and help you decide which coins to certify. Most authorized dealers are familiar with both services' standards and can warn you off submitting coins that are most likely headed for a "body bag" (due to damage).

If you live within driving distance of an authorized dealer, make an appointment to be sure he is available to preview them. If you are not within a reasonable driving distance, you may ship your coins to an authorized dealer of your choice. As this situation adds an additional element of trust, you should pick someone you feel is trustworthy. A good rule of thumb is to select an authorized dealer who is also a member of the Professional Numismatists Guild (PNG). The PNG is the most prestigious numismatic fraternal organization because each new candidate must undergo a detailed background check and be approved by the entire membership. They must then operate under a strict Code of Ethics and accept binding arbitration in the event of disputes. Contact information for the PNG is also included in the Appendix.

Declaring Submission Value for Insurance

When you prepare to submit your collectibles for grading, you will be asked to declare a value for insurance purposes in case the package is lost or the items are damaged either in transit or at the grading service. Since grading and shipping fees are impacted by this decision, you need to weigh the value ranges of the service levels with the likelihood of loss or damage, then select a liberal, yet realistic value for the items.

TIPS FOR HEIRS: As a non-collector, getting 3rd party grading for the significant items in your inheritance may give you a far greater comfort level in assessing the real value of the collection. Because you are probably unfamiliar with the "language" of the hobby, to say nothing of the nuances, we recommend that you spend additional time in qualifying the authorized dealer you consult. Speak plainly about your goals and ask lots of questions. If you're not sure about the meaning of an answer, don't hesitate to say so and ask for a more detailed explanation. You can't know too much about your inheritance; only knowing too little can hurt you.

CHAPTER eight

Having Your Collection Appraised

Appraisals of collectibles and other tangible personal property are an integral part of estate planning. Appraisals are required for estate tax, charitable contributions and gift tax purposes as well as insurance and divorce settlements.

A key element in the process is the choosing of an appraiser. In rare coins, for instance, the appraiser must be familiar with trends in the entire rare coin market as well as the individual specialization areas he or she may have in order to accurately provide appraisals that can be submitted to the IRS.

Most rare coins are easier to evaluate than most other forms of tangible assets due to the wide empirical database that exists. U.S. rare coins have independent pricing guides that are published weekly, recognized, independent certification services and a strong established auction history. However, some rare coins are rather esoteric and require a skilled appraiser to evaluate the factors of provenance, rarity, variety, type, quality and in cases of uncertified coins, the condition based on contemporary standards.

Appraising artwork and paper collectibles (rare books, comics, and art) often requires an appraiser with a keen eye for the works of particular artists and an acute understanding of the current market for those particular genres of the collectibles. It may be necessary to talk with several appraisers before finding one with the particular expertise that you seek.

It is also important that the appraiser be aware of the IRS rules governing appraisals as set forth in the Internal Revenue Code of 1986, the Treasury regulations promulgated under the Code and interpreting authority. Neither the IRS nor Congress has yet sought to unify the appraisal requirements for income tax, estate tax or gift tax purposes. Crucial differences exist, such as (1) the requirement that certain estate tax but not income tax or gift tax appraisals be made under oath, and (2) the minimum values (e.g. $3,000, $5,000 or $10,000) above which special appraisal requirements apply.

As a result, in contracting for an appraisal to be used for tax purposes, you should take care to state clearly the tax purpose for which the appraisal in being obtained. In addition, you should review the draft appraisal for compliance with the specific requirements.

The most common situations in which tangible personal property must be valued for tax purposes are:
- When a taxpayer claims a charitable deduction on his or her income tax return.
- When an executor values a decedent's personal effects.

- When a taxpayer reports the value of a gift on a gift tax return

Other purposes are discussed in the following paragraphs including regulations governing excess benefit transactions that involve certain exempt organizations. In each case the taxpayer or executor may be required to supply or rely upon an appraisal of the property. The specific requirements are different in each situation.

Income Tax Purposes

The most complicated of appraisal requirements are those demanded of a taxpayer claiming a charitable deduction. For any item of tangible personal property valued at over $5,000 the taxpayer must obtain a "Qualified Appraisal" and attach an "Appraisal Summary" to the income tax return. If any item is valued at over $20,000 the taxpayer must attach the Qualified Appraisal itself rather than the Appraisal Summary to the tax return.

The appraisal regulations under section 170 specify in detail the requirements of a Qualified Appraisal. These requirements are summarized in IRS Publication 561 "Determining the Value of Donated Property." Taxpayers and advisors should bear in mind that this publication is intended only for assistance in preparing income tax returns, not estate or gift tax returns.

The four general requirements of a Qualified Appraisal are as follows:

(A) It must be made not more than 60 days before the date of the contribution of the property to the charity and not later than the due date of the return on which a deduction for the contribution is claimed.

(B) No part of the fee for the appraisal can be based on a percentage of the appraised value of the property.

(C) It must be prepared and signed by a "Qualified Appraiser" and all appraisers who contribute to its preparation must also sign it.

(D) It must include:

  (1) A detailed description of the property from which someone who is not generally familiar with the type of property could recognize this particular item; for certified coins the description should include the certifying organization, such as PCGS, NGC or ANACS and the certification number on the case;

  (2) A description of the physical condition of the property. For certified coins the grade of the coin on the case is sufficient;

  (3) The date (or expected date) of contribution;

  (4) The terms of any agreement that the donor has entered into or expects to enter with regard to the property;

  (5) The name, address and taxpayer ID number of the Qualified Appraiser or Appraisers and if the Qualified Appraiser is employed or engaged as an independent contractor by another person or firm, the name, address and taxpayer ID number of that person or firm;

  (6) The qualifications of the Qualified Appraiser who signs the appraisal, including the appraiser's background, experience, education and any membership in professional appraisal associations;

(7) A statement that the appraisal was prepared for income tax purposes;

(8) The date or dates the property was valued;

(9) The appraised fair market value on the date of the contribution;

(10) The method of valuation used to determine the fair market value;

(11) The specific basis for the valuation;

(12) A description of the fee arrangement between the donor and appraiser.

The regulations under section 170 provide very detailed guidelines concerning the qualifications of a Qualified Appraiser. These guidelines are intended to ensure that the Qualified Appraiser is competent to make the appraisal and are sufficiently disinterested to be able to render an honest opinion of value. The regulations provide:

(A) Certain individuals are not allowed to be Qualified Appraisers, including:

(1) The donor of the property (or taxpayer who claims the deduction);

(2) The donee of the property;

(3) A party to the transaction in which the donor acquired the property, such as the person who sold the property to the donor, unless the donor makes the donation within two months of acquiring the property and claims an appraised value no higher than the price at which it was acquired;

(4) A person who regularly prepares appraisals for one of the above and who does not per-

form a majority of his or her appraisals for other persons;

(5) A person employed by or related to any of the above persons in (1), (2) or (3) above.

(B) A Qualified Appraiser must certify on the Appraisal Summary that he or she:

(1) Holds himself or herself out to the public as an appraiser, or performs appraisals on a regular basis;

(2) Is qualified to make appraisals of the type of property being valued because of the qualifications in the appraisal;

(3) Is not one of the excluded individuals named above;

(4) Is not receiving an appraisal fee based upon a percentage of the appraised property value; and

(5) Understands that there is a penalty for aiding and abetting under a statement of tax liability.

(C) A person cannot be a Qualified Appraiser if the donor has knowledge of facts that would cause a reasonable person to expect that the appraiser will overstate the value of the donated property.

A taxpayer who claims a charitable deduction greater than $500 must attach IRS Form 8283 to his or her income tax return and fill out Section A of the form, which requires information about the donated property and the donation. When a taxpayer claims a deduction for an item valued at more than $5,000, he or she must also fill out Section B of the form. Section B is the "Appraisal Summary."

The Appraisal Summary requires additional information about the donated property as well as the signature of the donee and a certification signed by the Qualified Appraiser containing the representations described above.

In 1996, the IRS issued Revenue Procedure 96-15, which provides the procedures through which a taxpayer may request from the IRS a binding (on the IRS and the taxpayer) "Statement of Value" as to any item of art that has been appraised at $50,000 or more. The taxpayer may then use the Statement of Value to substantiate the value of the property for income, estate or gift tax purposes.

A taxpayer who requests a Statement of Value to substantiate a charitable contribution of property must submit to the IRS a Qualified Appraisal, a required user fee of $2,500 and an Appraisal Summary. Because the taxpayer can request a Statement of Value only after the contribution has been made, the steps outlined in Revenue Procedure 96-15 may be of little practical use to the taxpayer.

A taxpayer seeking a Statement of Value for estate or gift tax purposes must submit to the IRS an appraisal containing certain specified information, a required user fee of $2,500, a description of the item, the appraised fair value of the item, the cost, date and manner of acquisition and the date of death (or alternate valuation date, if applicable) or the date of the gift. Again, obtaining a Statement of Value is often of little practical use to the taxpayer as it just accelerates review of values and is therefore not a help in planning.

Estate Tax Purposes

When an estate includes household and personal effects, the executor must file Schedule F of the estate tax return, itemizing the property and reporting its value. All items of property must be listed separately unless they have a value of less than $100. Items having a value less than $100 and contained in the same room on the date of death can be grouped together. As an alternative to itemizing, the executor may provide a written statement, prepared under penalties of perjury, setting forth the aggregate value of the property as appraised by competent appraisers of recognized standing and ability (or by dealers in the class of property involved).

As a practical matter, in large estates one or more appraisers value almost all "miscellaneous property." The reasons for this include (1) that the alternative to itemizing, mentioned above, requires that executors rely on appraisals by either a competent appraiser or a dealer, and (2) that the Internal Revenue Code prescribes penalties for both undervaluing and overvaluing estate property. These penalties may be waived on a showing of "reasonable cause and good faith," which may be demonstrated by justifiable reliance on a professional appraisal.

In determining whether reliance on a particular appraisal demonstrated "reasonable cause and good faith," the IRS will take into account: (1) the methodology and assumptions underlying the appraisal, (2) the appraised value, (3) the relationship between appraised value and purchase price, (4) the circumstances under which the appraisal was obtained, and (5) the appraiser's relationship to the taxpayer or to the activity in which the property is used.

Certain types of tangible personal property must be appraised separately, specifically, items having marked artistic or intrinsic value in excess of $3,000, such as jewelry, furs, silverware, paintings, etchings, antiques, books, vases, oriental rugs or coin and stamp collections. The appraisal of such items must be made by an "expert or experts" and it must be made under oath, an often overlooked requirement. The appraisal must also be accompanied by the executor's written statement, made under penalties of perjury, as to the completeness of the itemized list of such property and as to the disinterested character and the qualifications of the appraiser or appraisers.

The regulations provide little guidance regarding the preparation of estate tax appraisals. Otherwise, they merely provide guidance for appraisals of specific types of property:

(1) Books in sets by standard authors should be listed in separate groups;

(2) In listing paintings having artistic value, the size, subject, and artist's name should be stated;

(3) In the case of oriental rugs, the size, make, and general condition should be given; and

(4) In the case of silverware, sets of silverware should be listed in separate groups, groups of individual pieces of silverware should be weighed and the weights given in troy ounces and, in arriving at the value of silverware, the appraisers should take into consideration its antiquity, utility, desirability, condition and obsolescence.

Additional general and specific guidance for estate tax appraisals has been provided in Revenue Procedure 66-49, which suggests that, for general purposes, an appraisal report should contain as least the following:

(1) A summary of the appraiser's qualifications;

(2) A statement of value and the appraiser's definition of the value he obtained;

(3) The basis upon which the appraisal was made; and

(4) The signature of the appraiser and the date the appraisal was made.

Gift Tax Purposes

A taxpayer who makes a completed gift is required to file a gift tax return on IRS Form 709 and, except to the extent of a deduction such as the charitable or marital deduction, pay tax on the transfer at graduated rates based on the value of the gift if the gift generates a tax in excess of the unified credit amount.

The instructions for the gift tax return and the applicable regulations require that the taxpayer attach to the return either a detailed description of the method used to determine the fair market value of the gifted property or an appraisal of the gifted property.

The regulations provide specific guidance regarding the preparation of gift tax appraisals. Although fairly general and applicable to gifts of many types of property, the regulation specify that a gift tax appraisal contain the following information:

(1) The date of the gift;

(2) The date on which the gifted property was appraised and the purpose of the appraisal;

(3) A description of the gifted property;

(4) A description of the qualifications of the appraiser;

(5) A description of the appraisal process used;

(6) Any information considered in determining the appraised value;

(7) The appraisal procedures followed, and the reason that supports the analyses, opinion and conclusions reached in the appraisal;

(8) The valuation method used, the rationale for the valuation method, and the procedure used in determining the fair market value of the gifted property; and

(9) The specific basis for the valuation, such as specific comparable sales or transactions.

The regulations also specify that an individual who meets the following criteria must prepare a gift tax appraisal:

(1) Holds himself or herself out to the public as an appraiser, or performs appraisals on a regular basis;

(2) Is qualified to make appraisals of the type of property being valued because of his or her qualifications, as described in the appraisal; and

(3) Is not the donor or recipient of the property or member of the family of the donor or recipient (which includes spouses, ancestors, lineal descendants and spouses of lineal descendants) or any person employed by the donor, the recipient or a member of the family of either donor or recipient.

The rules for the appraisal of tangible personal property may seem complicated but can become critically important if the advisor engages an appraiser who is not thoroughly familiar with them. For this reason, an advisor should ensure that the appraiser has up-to-date knowledge of both appraisal formats and the marketplace in which the most sustainable comparable values can be found.

Insurance Appraisal

You should insure your collection whether you keep it in a safe-deposit box or at home, and particularly if you exhibit or trade portions of it at shows. Your insurance company will probably want an appraisal prior to granting coverage, but even if they don't, it may be in your best interests to secure one. The premiums will be assessed on your stated value, but should there be a claim and the research reveals the values were overstated, you will not get the degree of coverage you paid for. Just as with jewels, fine art, or furs, if you over-insure your property, all you accomplish is making the insurance company wealthier.

An insurance appraisal should be figured at replacement cost – the price you would have to pay if you went out and replaced the collection buying from dealers or at auction. It should not matter whether you paid $10,000 for the collection or $200,000; if it would cost $100,000 to replace it today, that's exactly how much you should insure it for. The pertinent point here is that this is a retail appraisal, probably the only instance in which that is most beneficial to the owner. You should make sure the appraiser understands that the purpose is for insurance, as most appraisals are for liquidation value.

Premiums vary by company, but by far, the cheapest coverage is in force when your collection is always in a safe-deposit box. This may seem unnecessary, but in the 1980s, a friend's substantial collection was stolen from his safe-deposit box when a large bank in Boston was broken into over the weekend. Rare, but it happens. Another client's bank vault was flooded for five entire days. Figure to pay one-half percent for annual safe-deposit box coverage ($500 for $100,000) and at least double that if you want coverage outside the bank. Special circumstances may require additional premiums, so read the policy language carefully for exceptions and ask any questions you feel are necessary for you to fully understand the policy.

Appraisal For Divorce

If you are getting a divorce and a collection is among the marital assets, you will most likely be required to get it appraised. Finances allowing, one party may want to keep the collection rather than have it sold and the proceeds divided. This could create one more conflict during the divorce. The spouse wanting to keep the collection will hope for a low appraisal, while the selling spouse will hope for a higher one. The fairest way to obtain a Divorce Appraisal is to take the collection to two or three reputable dealers (three is optimal, but may be unnecessary and expensive if the first two are within 20% of each other). Tell each dealer you need a written appraisal of what they would pay to buy the collection outright. Expect the appraisal/offer to have a time limit of as little as one week.

Assuming that the collection is not to be split up, a "one figure" appraisal (e.g. the sum total offer is $20,000) should be sufficient versus pages of individual offers that would increase the appraisal cost unnecessarily.

Selecting an Appraiser

Selecting the appraiser is the most important part of the process. In addition to the qualifications mentioned earlier, you are looking for someone who will represent your best interests in providing a knowledgeable and honest evaluation of your collection. Further, the evaluation should match the needs of the situation it is addressing.

That said, you still need to maintain the responsibility of looking out for your own interests.

If your collection is made up of coins, your appraiser should be a life member of the American Numismatic Association (ANA), a member of the Professional Numismatists Guild (PNG), be established for at least five years (and preferably ten) in the same area, have financial references from a reliable bank and have a solid reputation with knowledgeable collectors. This is ideal. Depending on your location and the relative value of your collection, you may choose (or have) to settle for less, but these are the qualifications you should be seeking. If you have a significant collection, it is probably in your best interests to incur higher expenses (if necessary) to engage an appraiser at this level. Remember, such expenses are usually deductible.

What Will it Cost?

A formal appraisal can be an expensive undertaking, but the important considerations are that it's done right and that the expense is appropriate relative to the value of the collection. Expect to pay $100 an hour on average. Some small town dealers charge $50 - $75 per hour, dealers in large cities or "high rent" districts tend to charge $125 - $150 per hour, so $100 is a good average. If the collection is significant and the material is rare or esoteric, or if the situation is complex or unusually contentious, you may need the services of a top-rate professional. Their rates can rival that of a law firm's $250 - $500 per hour. We would emphasize, however, that such a level of expertise is usually not necessary for most collections.

In qualifying a dealer, ask for an approximate charge after discussing the scope and purpose of the appraisal. If the dealer won't commit to a figure (say "2-3 hours, no more than 3," for example), find someone else who will. Remember, a "one price," liquidation appraisal will require a lot less time (and expense) than a line by line, individually-bid "grocery list." You may not even have to pay for the former at all. Some dealers will give you a dated, written offer to purchase your collectibles on a no-obligation basis. Unless you need insurance appraisal values, that offer would suffice as a liquidation appraisal. Others may charge you for a written appraisal with the proviso that if you sell them the collection by an arbitrary date, the appraisal fees will be rebated. Dealers would much rather buy collections than appraise them and you can use that leverage to your advantage. In all fairness, however, if someone does a "free" appraisal, you should at least give them the opportunity to bid when you make a decision to sell.

Safety of Collectibles During Appraisal

It is your responsibility to ensure the safety of your collection during the appraisal. You should expect it to cost more, but once you have selected an appraiser, the safest method is to have the appraiser come to your bank. A true professional will make an inventory if one does not already exist and then make evaluation notes right there in the tiny safe-deposit room. The appraiser will then take the notes back to his office to determine values and assemble the appraisal. Tell the appraiser when you need it, and don't forget to ask for an estimate on time. Even a modest collection, appraised under these ideal conditions (ideal for you, but NOT necessarily for the dealer) will probably be charged at several hours.

A less expensive alternative is to take the collectibles to the dealer and sit with them while the appraisal notes are being made, returning at an agreed upon date to pick up the appraisal. If your location or schedule requires you to either ship or leave your collection for appraisal, you should put a little more effort into qualifying your appraiser. This is simply good business and a natural step in assuring the safety of your collection.

In summary, determine the scope of your collection and what you are trying to accomplish with an appraisal, select the professional who combines the qualifications and economies best suited to your situation, and safeguard your collection during the process.

TIPS FOR HEIRS: If you have created a basic inventory where none existed previously, try to get a "ball park" estimate of the collection's worth in your initial discussion with potential appraisers. Because the condition of any collectible is such an issue, they may be reluctant. They should, however, be able to tell if you're dealing with a few hundred, a few thousand, or something of greater value. That information should help you gauge the economies of the process. At that point, we would recommend that you spend a little more time qualifying your appraiser if you are not a collector and are unfamiliar with "who's who" in the marketplace.

PART four

Disposing of Your Collection

CHAPTER nine

Selling Your Collection Through Outright Sale

"Liquidation price means low enough that the buyer feels comfortable even with items he didn't want."

This chapter is the first of three that outline methods for disposing of your collection. Each has benefits for certain types of collectibles, and weaknesses for others. The common thread is that each method subscribes to the philosophy that "time is money." This means that, all other things being equal, the faster you get paid for your collection, the less you are likely to receive. This is not an unfair situation, as you will see in these chapters. We are going to try to put you inside the heads of your potential customers, and  help you understand their motivations for buying. Their time is valuable, as is yours. Our goal is to aid you in making a measured decision about the amount of time you are willing to invest in the disposition process.

Outright sale is without question the easiest method of selling a whole or partial collection. You present the articles to one or more buyers. They make offers. You either accept or decline. Your time invested is limited to the period you are with the collectibles at the evaluation(s); if you accept an offer, you receive your payment and get on with your life. If you assembled the collection, this may either be devastating or cathartic, but it won't drag out.

First, we will assume that you are offering any collection of substance to a dealer in that collectible type. Dealers are most likely to have both the motivation and wherewithal to buy an entire collection. It is also easier to locate them through their advertising and they can be qualified through their references and affiliations. What is the dealer thinking when you bring him your collection to bid?

Dealers are in business to buy collections coming through the front door (or through the mail). Most of their advertising and their longevity at a particular site are planned specifically to entice just such a situation. Many collectibles are a fixed-supply commodity. If you're in the business, you have to acquire products to sell, and advantageous buying is at the core of such a business. The dealer wants to buy your collection – it's his raison d'être – and the nicer the collection, the more he wants it.

We have two parties together; one who wants to sell and one who wants to buy. Now comes the sticking point. In any trading situation, the final result reflects the combination of knowledge and leverage of the parties. The dealer wants to buy the collection at the lowest price he can pay without it walking out the door. His leverage is that he has the money and willingness to buy the whole deal, plus any degree of impatience that you possess or he can instill in you. You may also believe that he is more knowledgeable about current markets than you are. You, nonetheless, want to feel that you are getting the maximum reasonable price for your collectibles. Your leverage is that he does not want to let you out the door with the collection. Your knowledge and negotiating skills are also an advantage.

A dealer is bidding on three planes when a collection is offered. First, there are those items for which he knows he has customers or which are readily liquid in his retail or "high wholesale" operations. These will generally be figured strongly because his risk and expense of holding inventory is minimal. Second are the articles that do not fit that criteria—collectibles that are not routinely traded and which will require greater effort to sell. This particularly applies to bulk where additional shipping weight is also a factor. Such items will be figured cheaply because of the effort and expense necessary to resell them at a profit. This may seem callous, but it's a matter of perspective. Some of your collectibles may be very special to you. Those same pieces sitting unsold on a dealer's shelf are merely inventory that is losing (or costing) interest. He will take the time to find the "high buyer" because it's how he makes his living, but his bid for those items will reflect both his intent to make a profit at wholesale, and any uncertainty about the high buyer and his buying levels. The third factor is not related to the collectibles, but rather what the dealer perceives his competition to be. If you live in a small town with only one dealer (in the field of your collectible), his basic assumption may be that he pretty much has things his own way. This may also apply in any locale if the dealer perceives you aren't "shopping." His bid will not be competitive.

There are those who will read the last paragraph and mumble about "rip-off" dealers, but the reality is endemic throughout society and business in general, not just this portion of it; it lies at the very heart of Capitalism. Americans as a whole are not raised to function in a barter system or to be negotiators. We go to the store and buy what we want at the marked price, only sometimes, perhaps, after checking the newspapers for sales. It's what we see in childhood and by the time we are adults making our own decisions, most of us are conditioned to the process. As a result, a large percentage of people still pay "sticker price" even in those environments where some negotiating is expected.

When selling or trading something in, the same conditioning applies – the dealer establishes the market and as the perceived authority figure, a surprisingly large number of people accept that quote as fact—or at least believe that their only options are yes or no. The dealer, of course, falls into that group of people who, through aptitude or training, are both comfortable and practiced in negotiating (that is, appearing not to be negotiating). Naturally, you need to present your collection and your business skills in their best light if you want to get a better price for your coins.

Here are some tips for negotiating the best deal on your collection:

- **Know the Best Items for Direct Sale**
 To get the best prices from direct sale, consider all of the following tips and how you might apply them to your effort.
- **Allow yourself a National Marketplace**
 The world has become a much smaller place through increasingly more rapid communications and transport. You need not limit your search for outlets to your hometown. If your collection is significant enough, the outlets will come to you!

Find a "Full Service" Dealer
 Remember the note about liquidity-based bidding. A large dealer with a wide clientele and business contacts will "see" your more common items as more liquid because they routinely sell that kind of material as well as the "good" collectibles. They already know who the high buyers are and what they're paying. Additionally, because of their business volume, they will not have the need (or temptation) to "make their month" on your collection. As a result, they're more likely to bid the whole deal "closer."

Create an "Aura of Competition"
 It is rarely a bad idea to get more than one bid on something you're selling and NEVER a bad idea to let a potential buyer know that other people are bidding (whether they are or not). This can be communicated after you get a bid – "Is this your best offer, Mr. Smith? I know dealers sometimes leave a little 'wiggle room,' but I have two other people bidding and this isn't that kind

of negotiation" – or before – "I want you to know in advance, Mr. Smith, that I'm offering the collection for bid to three people. Please give me your best offer the first time."

Display Your Knowledge in Discussing the Bid

Dealers and people handling collectibles respect those who speak the language. You don't necessarily have to have a deep knowledge if you can "sell" yourself on a few key points. If you have a few pieces in your collection that stand out, bring them up. "What do you bid for this, Mr. Smith?" Similarly, you should get a feel for the levels being offered for your second tier material.

"Play the Player"

You needn't be a market expert to get the "feel" of a collection if you are at all adept at reading others. Follow up the responses to the questions above with further questions. "You bid ____? Isn't that a little low?" If the dealer can immediately address the questions with logic and weigh options, he may be extremely glib, but more likely he is comfortable with his offer. Alternatively, if he's evasive or there's no logic to his response, there's very likely negotiating room left in the offer.

Split the Deal

Rather than offer the whole collection in one lot, offer "test" groups for bid to get a feel for your potential buyers. Generally, there is more control when dealing with smaller, manageable "pieces" and you can often get a bit more in this manner. There is also the "bait" technique of letting the bidders know that there is more beyond. This perception may lead some bidders to treat you better in the early rounds. The trade-off is more of your time.

In summary, only you can decide how much of your time you are willing to invest in the disposition of your collection. Generally, the more productive time spent, the better the result. You can be most effective in preparing for disposition by knowing your collection, knowing the market and knowing your potential buyers.

TIPS FOR HEIRS: If you are a non-collector and after reading this chapter you want to use this method, we would recommend strongly that you seek multiple offers. We would also recommend that you first read and consider the options in the next two chapters as well.

CHAPTER ten

Selling Your Collectibles Through an Agent

"A good agent is a true blessing."

It may be practical for you or your heirs to use the services of an agent to sell your collection. The objective in choosing this method is to get more money than you would through direct sale. The trade-off (again) is that it will take more time. That said, you might even wish to enlist the services of several agents to sell different parts of your collection.

Many people employ an agent to assist them in selling real estate. The agent knows real estate values, has ways to contact qualified customers, and understands how to deal with them. A good dealer has the same qualifications and contacts in his field, but you rarely hear the term 'agent' used in that context. Dealers would generally prefer to purchase collections outright (at the lower price), and then have a free hand to resell them without customer consultation. They may, however, take a collection on consignment rather than let it walk out the door.

A client/agent relationship is a relatively long one. As the owner of multiple properties may commission the real estate agent to dispose of one at a time, so may the owner of a collection turn over its elements in groups. This gives the agent a more narrow focus to concentrate on and allows you to maintain control. The key in any case is regular communication and interaction between you and the agent. Items that the agent has been given may not sell and must be returned. The asking price may need to be adjusted downward. There may be a change in market conditions. While the agent may be doing most of the work, you, the seller, will need to stay involved. As real estate agents and sellers work together as partners to their mutual benefit, so must you and your agent. The agent should be expected to inform you of market conditions and help set prices. Above all, you must be able to trust the agent; to have faith in his ability; and be confident that he is looking after your best interests. One way to gauge this is to test the agent's overall performance with a few collectibles prior to making any major commitment.

An agent is not worth the trouble unless he can get 10% to 25% more than you could get in a direct sale. Remember, the agent's role is not just to know the collectibles, but also the markets and the players.

The first step in seeking an agent is to determine the nature of what you plan to sell, then try to match the agent with the product. This may seem obvious, but a common mistake among sellers is to retain unqualified agents. If your pieces are specialized, seek a specialist. If they are mainstream, look for the following kinds of qualifications:

- **Scope of Company**

  The agent (or his company) routinely handles articles of the same type, condition and values as those in your collection, and has strong customer demand for them.

- **Grading Service Experience**

  In the case of coins, the agent (or his company) routinely submits coins to the grading services and has a strong feel for where the "standard lines" of the grades are. Ideally, the agent or other personnel in his company will have worked for a grading service and understand both the process and "looks" that are most often rewarded on marginal decisions.

- **Regular Show Attendance**

  The agent (or his company) attends shows on a regular basis where routine contact with other collectors and dealers provides a feel for the market and provides a wide range of business contacts. Taken a step further, attendance at national shows would give even more insight and opportunity.

- **Mailing List**

  The agent (or his company) has an extensive mailing list and will present your collection to the maximum number of potential buyers.

These qualifications promise the potential of significantly higher returns, but you also want to pick an agent who genuinely wants the role. A lot of dealers only want to buy and sell collectibles, and really don't have the time or inclination to work with you as an agent. You should not be upset if someone you approach turns you down, nor do you want to enlist a reluctant ally. The last thing you need is a dealer who thinks he's doing you a favor by selling your pieces for you.

Many variables can influence the arrangement you make; however, five important elements should be negotiated in any event:
- The agent's fees should be discussed and agreed upon in advance. Generally, the agent should receive a percentage of the selling price. This fee is usually graduated and predicated on the value of the collectibles. You could hardly expect an agent to go to the trouble and expense of selling a $100 item for a 5% commission. A more equitable arrangement might be a 15% commission on pieces valued under $1000 and 10% on articles valued over that amount. That, of course, is a matter of negotiation. A firm minimum price for each item or group of items to be sold should be agreed upon in advance with the understanding that the seller be advised before any articles are sold for less than this fixed price. Turning a collection over to an agent and accepting a promise to do his best is not acceptable. It could also be expected that the agent might do some research and make a few phone calls prior to suggesting a minimum price. Agents should be prepared to substantiate the values they suggest. Conversely, you should not demand unreasonable minimums. No agent is going to waste his time and energy trying to sell articles that are obviously overpriced. Negotiating the minimums is a critical component of this kind of arrangement. If you are not comfortable with the value range of your individual collectibles, it may be best to get a written offer first. Then

you'll know what you're trying to improve upon before negotiating with an agent.

The agent should be given the exclusive right to sell the collection for a specific period of time. Depending on the nature of the collection, the agent may have standard practices he wishes to follow. Allowing the agent a set length of time to sell the collection should be separated from the payment schedule. Within reason, the owner should be paid as the items are sold. A good method to use is to make periodic settlements based on time or dollar amount. If the agent is given 90 days to sell the collection, it would seem fair to request that he makes payments at thirty and sixty day intervals, or when the amount collected reaches $5000 or more. We would be wary of an agent who didn't agree to this proposal. Requesting periodic payments is also a simple and positive way to measure the agent's performance.

- The agent must agree to be totally responsible for the collection while it is in his possession. The agent you select may be the most honorable person on earth, but he would still not be immune to theft or natural disaster. Proof of sufficient insurance coverage is mandatory. In many cases, the most prudent plan would still be to give the agent a limited number of your collectibles to sell at any one time.

- Put the agreement in writing. Good contracts make good trading partners, and this is a business arrangement between two parties. All terms must be spelled out and the document signed by both parties in whatever manner creates a binding contract in your state.

One other area where agents can be used is in moving "bulk" coins. Bulk is the bane of most coin dealers' existences. Some coin collectors accumulated ten proof and mint sets a year for forty years and can't understand why the dealer is not enthused when the three wheel barrows full of sets roll through the door. The answers are low price and low margin plus high (relative) weight. We can virtually guarantee you that if you have a lot of this material in your collection, it will generally be bid very low as part of any outright purchase offer— probably 70% to 85% of "sheet." From the dealer's perspective, it is cumbersome, difficult to process and likely to sit gathering dust while more lucrative sales of products are prioritized. Nonetheless, there are a few dealers who specialize in the sale of this kind of material and are the "high buyers." Your agent for this kind of material should know who those high buyers are and be willing to handle the administrative functions of arranging and completing the transactions. In return, he should either receive a mutually agreed fixed fee or perhaps 5% - 10% and expenses. You should still come out ahead of the typical direct sale offer.

In summary, match the agent with the material, establish realistic minimums that make using this method worthwhile, qualify the agent, put the agreement in writing and communicate regularly with the agent throughout the agreement period.

TIPS FOR HEIRS: If you are a non-collector and wish to use this option, we recommend that you get an outright purchase offer first. Use extra diligence in qualifying potential agents, and pay close attention in having the agent(s) validate the established minimum prices. Use the direct offers as a comparison and make sure that the minimums offer a significant increase. It may be even more important here to offer small test groups to get comfortable with the process and the agent.

CHAPTER eleven

Selling Your Collection at Auction

The ideal situation for selling any product is to get it in front of as many potential customers as possible. When the product is rare competing customers are important, and an auction is frequently the best venue. There are many benefits to this method of disposition, but the primary one is that in a good auction (one with many bidders), each item should realize at least its true worth.

The auction is a true free market in which each article stands on its own merits. Every item is examined carefully by those people most interested in it and are willing to back their opinions with money. If you have a collectible that is rare  enough that it trades infrequently, its current value would have to be described as uncertain. In an outright purchase of such an item, most dealers will factor that uncertainty into their price unless they absolutely know they have a buyer at a certain level. A well-advertised sale by an established auction house, on the other hand, will likely draw the attention of all the known buyers—and any others as well. The collector community is generally a small one, and most serious buyers are aware when something of interest is offered for sale, particularly at auction. When that condition exists, competitive demand will dictate the strongest result and produce the truest value for a given collectible.

Another competitive bidding factor is eye-appeal. All collectibles were not created equal and many people will pay a premium for pieces they consider superior.

Finally, if you have something esoteric – items that are not traded routinely– a good auction may again bring the very best price. If you have substantial holdings of such, choose an auctioneer with a strong track record for the particular genre – one who has the clientele (both mailing list and attendance) and auction locations to put the collection in front of the greatest number of potential buyers.

These factors are what make an auction the best venue for a wide spectrum of collectibles. Your task is to pick the auctioneer that can put your pieces in front of the right people, preferably in quantity. When looking for an auctioneer, you should consider the following qualifications:

- **Financial Resources**

    An auction consignment is first and foremost a business deal. As with using an agent, an auctioneer must demonstrate sufficient financial resources to ensure your comfort that they can both mount a sale and pay you at the stated settlement date. They must also accept liability and provide full insurance against the loss or damage of your collection.

- **Longevity in the Business**

    The auction is a multi-faceted business operation that requires a great deal of development before everything flows smoothly: consignor and bidder bases, cataloging references and expertise, site setup and physical security, auction flow and administrative efficiency and much, much more. Practice makes perfect is doubly applicable here, because it's your money that's involved. Go with a proven entity.

- **Advertising Resources**
  Success breeds success. You can't have the top sales without great advertising and vice versa. Look for the companies who are doing the major advertising in the trade papers and on the Internet. They put on the sales that justify the cost of full-page ads and, the bigger the sale, the more buyers to bid on your coins.

- **Location**
  A company that is limited to holding auctions in locations out of the mainstream is just not going to draw a large bidder base. Some companies hold auctions in major financial centers with good regional access, while others appropriately utilize the broad reach of the Internet.

- **Competitive Rates**
  Auction companies charge both buyer's and seller's fees to pay the expenses of the sale and turn a profit. A seller's fee of 15% has become standard and you should not have to pay more, unless your collection has extraordinary "bulk" or requires out-of-the ordinary attention. Indeed, if you have a significant collection, you may be able to negotiate a better rate.

- **Strong Writing and Imagery**
  Catalog descriptions and photography create immediate excitement and demand for a sale's collectibles and are all that is available to entice bidders who can-

not attend the sale in person. Our company, Heritage Galleries, is currently pioneering the use of CD-ROM and the Internet as alternative cataloging media, and this may well become the wave of the future. Until then, look for examples of good catalog writing and high quality photography.

- **Professional Personnel**

    It takes quality personnel and lots of them to put on a great auction. The auction process is a complex one when done right. Consignment coordination, grading advice, cataloging, customer relations are all important factors. In qualifying auctioneers, be sure to ask them how many people are involved in handling your consignment and what their roles are. Our company provides potential consignors with a video that details the auction process from start to finish, and other companies should at least have literature that covers the same ground. Any company is only as good as its people. Talk to several and get a feel for how they will treat your collection. In summary, auction is often the best venue for high-quality collectibles, particularly if the items trade infrequently. A good auction draws the right mix of bidders to establish the real value for each individual piece, often far in excess of the average price.

    If this seems the best route for you, interview potential auctioneers to determine who combines the best business resources, venues and personnel assets.

    As an aside, our company has expanded our scope of venues to include several kinds of Internet auctions. The Internet is an amazing communications tool that, among other things, allows individuals to perform functions that previously were available only to businesses.

Someone asked, "What if a collector or heir wants to sell a collection by himself on the Internet?" Well, the many auction Web sites such as eBay, Yahoo and Amazon are certainly available for just such a project. The question is whether the choice is a good one relative to the other options. We have a good idea of the basics, so consider the following questions:

- Do you already have a "feedback" rating that will give you credibility with the bidder base? Many Internet auction bidders are leery about dealing with strangers. They are, after all, sending their hard-earned money to someone they've never met and probably never heard of. The equalizer is the feedback system that each Internet auction employs to establish "cyber-reputations." Each party to a "trade" gets the forum to comment on how the other trader performed. Every positive comment equals a point. Every complaint takes one away and the text of the complaint is there for future potential traders to evaluate. If you don't have a feedback rating, some bidders will avoid your auctions altogether and others will bid less (as if ameliorating their risk).

- Do you have the equipment and skill to create digital images of the articles to be auctioned? It's a proven fact that Internet auction items that don't have pictures bring much less money. Disregarding the skills, you will need either a high-resolution digital camera or a flatbed scanner, and an image management program to acquire the images. You will also need either a Web site or learn to use one of the "free posting" sites to upload your images.

- Do you have the skills to write descriptions for each item? Auction bidders are best motivated when a "story" is available to make the collectible more interesting. It's called "building value," and the visual image and description provide the combination that maximizes an Internet auction's results.
- Do you have the business skills to analyze potential problem situations? Can you collect a bad check or determine whether a "special request" from a customer is legitimate or a scam? Most of the people on the Internet are honest, but there are exceptions. Unfortunately, it doesn't take many bad deals to turn a profitable situation into a loss.
- Do you have the knowledge and resources to send high-dollar packages to a hundred different people? There is a lot of administrative responsibility in conducting one's own auctions, not the least of which is delivering the goods. It takes a thorough knowledge of postal regulations and requirements, a considerable amount of shipping materials and insurance, and a great deal of organization.
- Do you really want to sell collectibles that might have upgrade potential in an Internet-only venue? Actually, the question is whether you can recognize the pieces that have upgrade potential.

The final questions are whether you have the time and patience to accomplish this, and whether the outcome is likely to be superior enough to justify your added involvement (which will be considerable). If you can answer yes to all these questions, then maybe this is an option for you to consider and you probably don't need any further guidance from us. If not, we strongly recommend you seek a different option, as these questions just scratch the surface of what can be a complex and diverse process.

TIPS FOR HEIRS: A major auction can be the best option for heirs faced with the disposition of a valuable collection, particularly if you have no knowledge of collectibles and are concerned about getting fair value. In this scenario, the auctioneer is working on percentage and your best interests are theirs: the more money you make, the more money they make. Additionally, the values will be established by third parties in the competitive bidding process. The real benefit of employing a major auction house is their versatility. Summing up all of the methods of disposition, certain collectibles are better suited for one method, while others would benefit more from a different venue. A major company should be willing to recommend the best venue for each of your pieces and split the collection to your best advantage. Just be sure to ask.

CHAPTER twelve

Etiquette & Tips

"Tact is the ability to insult someone in such a manner as to have them leave smiling."

The purpose of this book is to help you plan for the future and, if you wish, to help you dispose of your collection without getting taken advantage of by the government, dealers or other collectors.

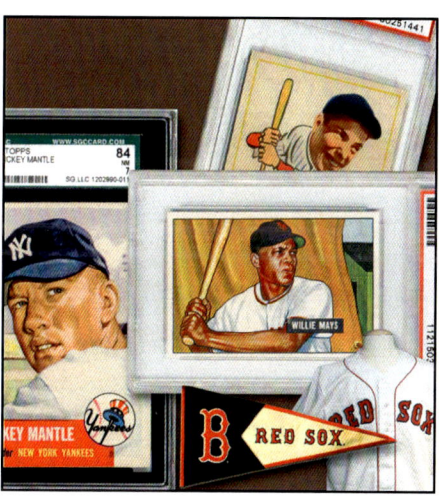

It is reasonable to assume that you want to receive as much money for your collection as possible. Similarly, it's reasonable to believe that potential buyers would want to pay the least amount they can. The one thing that's absolutely certain is that everyone else will prioritize his or her own interests. You should too. In plain language, it is your ultimate responsibility to make your best deal at some level. Once that's understood, a combination of business and common sense along with a little diplomacy will usually result in an acceptable compromise.

There are certain rules of etiquette within any collectibles community. The first premise is the division of roles. If you present yourself as a dealer, you are automatically responsible for all your actions and decisions in the arena of that collectible. That means if you make a mistake, you live with it. It also imparts a certain level of responsibility toward those who are not dealers. Dealers trade with each other at wholesale levels, in part because they speak a sort of verbal shorthand that assumes a level of expertise. A collectible is presented, offered, inspected and purchased (or not) without fanfare, and the principals move on to the next deal.

Conversely, many collectors ask a lot of questions (and rightly so), are nervous about their acquisitions, and return a portion of those purchases after the sale. In return for this extra "maintenance," dealers charge collectors more and pay them less than they would another dealer. It is the way of things, and perfectly justifiable, as there have to be both retail and wholesale levels for any market to function. Naturally, most collectors would like to purchase at wholesale, and occasionally, they get that opportunity. Usually, the key to this is demonstrating a familiarity with wholesale market levels, negotiating pleasantly and well, and asking only pertinent questions.

The same is true on the selling end. If you give the impression that you know what you are doing—are organized, prepared and unlikely to waste the dealer's time—you will get the best bid or options the first time out. We recommend, however, that you do not represent yourself as a dealer. Some collectors claim to be "vest pocket" dealers in hopes of receiving higher offers. Usually, this backfires as the dealer then feels relieved from any obligation to point out unrecognized rarities, or other possible advantages. Be who you are, be up front, and be positive.

Any dealer bidding your collection is being offered a valued opportunity to conduct his business. As a non-professional, you should be able to expect:

- An appointment with sufficient time to evaluate your collection.
- Financial and industry references at your request (and you should request them).
- Professional treatment of you and your collection with a mind to both care and security.
- You should ask (prior) that any items bid at $1,000 or more be identified singly, also that any article that would benefit from certification be listed.
- A written offer presented in a timely manner. The offer should be dated and any deadline noted.
- If the company has an auction house as well and you request it, recommendations on which collectibles are better suited for auction or direct sale should also be listed.
- Prompt payment in good funds if the offer is accepted. If the collection is sold at auction, payment in good funds on the settlement date as promised.

The dealer has a right to expect certain conduct from you as well:

- That you keep any scheduled appointment and are prompt. This applies to the dealer and his staff as well.
- The collection should be as organized as possible to minimize the time necessary to evaluate and bid it. Even a basic inventory indicating the location of each

item is helpful. If the collection lends itself to grouping, this should be done beforehand. If one group out of the collection contains most of the "value," it can be presented separately.

- You should not "shop" the dealer's offer to other dealers. It's OK to tell each bidder that other bids are being sought, but you should neither reveal what the other bids are nor the details of who is bidding. Shopping an offer for a few more bucks is strictly "bush league" and it can definitely backfire. For example, if your first bidder did not make a strong bid and you reveal the number, the second bidder may play the competition instead of the real value and you'll come up short. Similarly, if you reveal the identity of those you plan to see, the bidders could collude to your disadvantage. Remember, the aura of unknown competition is the strongest leverage you have to inspire dealers to figure the deal closely and give their best bids.

- You should tell the dealer "yes" or "no" in a reasonable amount of time, and that applies even if you accept another bid. It would be considerate for you to let him know the winning bid. He can learn from the experience and not feel that his time was wasted. That can be to your advantage as well, because if you bring back more collectibles for him to bid, he should both appreciate your professionalism and bid higher the next time.

Above all, you should both expect and extend courtesy. Neither waste time with a dealer who is discourteous, nor waste time responding. Ask and answer questions, but beware of becoming agitated, even if you disagree with something you hear. Your mission is to get the greatest possible price for your collection, and to accomplish that, it's usually best to reserve judgment until all the information is in. The very person you disagreed with may be the highest overall bidder.

As stated before, auction is often the most compelling option for collection disposition. A successful auction achieves the highest gross result for each lot when presented to a wide number of knowledgeable bidders, and especially when your collectibles are of choice quality. Still, there may be some items where your net result would have been better served in another venue. There is also the fact that many portions of an auction agreement are flexible and should be negotiated. Here are some of the issues and options:

- Ask the auctioneer's consignment coordinator to evaluate your collection and make recommendations on which articles should be auctioned and which would be better sold by another method. Ask him to explain why.
- Do you wish to be recognized for your collecting achievements? Some consignors prefer anonymity, but if you wish the recognition, becoming a signature consignor involves three factors:
  1. Your overall collection must be of general significant value. This could vary from auction to auction, but for a rough figure, let's use $250,000.
  2. Alternatively, you may have an interesting collection of a more specific focus—possibly all items are in one group or category. Don't hesitate to ask, particularly if there's a good story behind the collection!
- Auction companies charge a seller's fee and a buyer's fee to make their expenses and earn a profit. They are motivated to get as much for your collectibles as possi-

ble because they, in turn, will realize greater commissions. With that philosophy in mind, it is then a matter of resources expended on presenting and selling lots. If you have high-dollar, highly desirable single pieces, the auctioneer is much better off than if you have more inexpensive items, even if the total dollar value is the same. Therefore, you might be able to negotiate a lower seller's fee if you have the "right" kind of material. Other factors also apply. You should, for example, keep in mind that the lowest commission rate is not necessarily the best deal. The first consideration should be the auctioneer's capability to give your collection maximum exposure and promotion. Saving an extra percentage point or two is meaningless if another auctioneer could get an extra 20% for your collection.

- Some people sell their collectibles unrestricted and others place a "reserve" bid to protect them from bringing what they perceive to be "too little." We believe you should place reserve bids only if you are very familiar with current markets and have good reason to believe that you will easily realize more than the reserve elsewhere if you "buy-back" the lot. Auctioneers also have "reserve" fees, a percentage that you will pay if you do not let the item sell. These are necessary because the auctioneers must make money for their services and a lot that does not sell is a lost opportunity otherwise. Generally, the percentage is based on the overall terms of your consignment and how realistic the auctioneer perceives your reserves to be. You should expect the reserve fee to be 5%-10%. If the amount is more than that, ask for an explanation. If the consignment coordinator says your reserve is too high, you should discuss the rationale carefully. Consignment coordinators are usually very savvy about what works at what levels. If you don't heed their advice, you are gambling at best. Unless you're right, the auctioneer will still earn the reserve fee. You, on the other hand, will still have the article, but at a higher cost basis. Depending on the overall quality of your consignment, you may be able to negotiate better reserve terms on some or all of your collectibles.

- Ask the consignment coordinator for the cost of photography and lotting in the auctions you are considering. You want the maximum number of photographs and as much descriptive cataloging as possible, and this may vary depending on how much the auctioneer has to pay for the auction venue rights. For example, in some sales, the minimum value for a catalog photograph may be $1,500 and in others, $2,500. The latter sale, while possibly a better venue overall, might not be as good for your pieces valued $1,500 - $2,400. Similarly, each sale will have a minimum lot value. In some cases, it's $250, some $500, and in the very best of sales, it may be $1,000. Most auction companies will allow you to combine items to reach the minimum, but there is a limit to the number that may be used and still get individual, mainstream placement. The key point for you to remember here is that if your overall consignment is a good one, you may be able to negotiate a more lenient lot and photography standard.

- If you have "Large Lots" of coins, you need to work out the best arrangement to sell your coins to them profitably. Remember the rolls of "Wheat pennies" you accumulated by date and mintmark over the years?

How about the five proof sets you ordered from the Mint each year for the last three decades? Or the cheaper coins that you religiously stapled into 2 by 2s and stored in fourteen different stock boxes—sound familiar? We understand that all of these purchases contributed to your collecting pleasure, but we have one question to ask: would you travel somewhere else in the country to buy them today? The answer is almost certainly, "no," and that answer applies to others as well. As discussed previously, it is the "cream" of a collection that is most likely to "over-perform" at a major auction. Large lots are at the other end of the spectrum. It's a matter of logistics. By their very nature, large lots are bulky, cumbersome to carry to auction sites and heavy to ship once sold. They are time-consuming to catalog and require a lot of extra effort to earn the same percentage as a single coin of comparable lot value. Auction company personnel are not very fond of the large lots in major auctions and neither are most bidders, because their focus is on the more "high-powered" lots. Auctioneers will take your large lots for a big sale, but you have absolutely no leverage, and that's not what auctions are all about. In most cases, you would be better off asking the auctioneer to bid the large lots straight up. You will probably realize greater net proceeds and get paid immediately.

Our company has an additional option, primarily for coin collectors; Heritage holds "large lot only" sales. They are not elaborate and the lots are not extensively written-up. What these auctions do get is a bidder base of the country's strongest buyers of large lot material. These are dealers who specialize in inexpensive (relatively) coins, sets and bulk. We know who they are and they are fiercely competitive. We actually invite them to our offices three to five times annually (for the last decade) to buy the remnants of our collection purchases. They are frequently amazed at the items we have in-house for upcoming auctions. Now, we are taking consignments and letting the public in on this "well kept" secret. You do have to wait a bit longer for auction and settlement than with an outright sale, but it can be well worth it.

Occasionally, people ask us why they shouldn't dispose of their collectibles to or through another collector. The premise, of course, is that the collector would pay more and the playing field would be more level. There is some general merit to those statements, but there are some caveats as well:

- A collector will pay more for some items, but will rarely pay more for all of them. Take care that you don't get a bit more for the best few pieces of your collection only to find that nobody wants what's left.

- Being a collector in and of itself is no guarantee that the individual you contact is any more or less knowledgeable or moral than a dealer. We think on average, dealers would be better informed on current market conditions, upgrade potential and the reputations of potential buyers. We know of at least one situation where a collector acquaintance sold a collection for heirs, only to take a bad check from the buyer. That individual was well known as a "bad egg" by the dealer community, but the collector/agent was totally unaware. It took more than a year and considerable expense for the heirs to collect a fraction of the amount owed.

- As an agent, the collector is less likely to have insurance coverage for your collection while in his care. If you use a collector, don't forget to verify this just as you would with a dealer.

The bottom line is that you should qualify a collector in the same manner as you would a dealer. While you may see some advantages in such a relationship, don't overlook dealer advantages that you may be taking for granted. Although collectors may have good intentions, a major collection should be sold only with the help of a qualified professional. It's unwise to rely on a part-time hobbyist to dispose of a major financial asset. In most cases you would be better off to let the collector bid at auction against tens of thousands of others.

The final issues of etiquette are the relationships between a collector and his heirs, and between the heirs themselves. The collector, as the owner, has all the rights and responsibilities for the collection in his lifetime, and can provide guidance (or not) to his heirs as he sees fit. That said, any guidance (as opposed to none) is often a blessing. Even if only one or a portion of the heirs has any interest in the collectibles, a general understanding by all where they fit into the picture goes a long way towards familial harmony. The collector should identify and detail specific bequests if that is desirable. "Dad split them up that way in the will" is a lot more powerful than "I'm sure Dad wanted me to have this one." Similarly, the collector should indicate who should be contacted to help dispose of the collection—and who should not. It's amazing how many "old friends" can appear after the death of a known collector. The Executor, whether he or she is a family member or not, should be advised of all these details.

Heirs should remember that the other heirs are also probably under a great deal of stress, so be considerate of each other. We like to think that family is the most important thing, so here are some tips to avoid controversy if the collection needs to be split or disposed of equitably when specific guidance was not provided.

Leave the division to a third party. If the collection is not to be sold, have the appraiser break the inventory into the appropriate number of groups by value. If one or more heirs want specific pieces, have the appraiser value those individually and if the remainder of the collection is sold, use those amounts to adjust shares accordingly. Finally, if the collection is to be disposed of, but each heir wants "something" to remember the deceased by, determine the dollar value you want set aside and have each heir "buy" the collectibles they want at the appraised price. In all cases, remember to keep things in perspective. The collection once provided a great deal of pleasure to your loved one, and if there is any sentiment to be attached to them, it should be a positive one.

This has been a difficult handbook to prepare. There are two main reader groups, neither of whom should be happy at the implications of needing to read it. If you are a collector, the thought of estate planning may make you look closer at your own mortality than you wanted to. If a current heir, you've probably read this because your loved one declined to face that reality and left you a burden along with the inheritance.

We would take more pleasure in relating a more upbeat subject, but will be satisfied if this handbook has made things a little easier for you in addressing a difficult task. In closing, we offer this final guidance regardless of your circumstance or role:

1. Determine your goal.
2. Know your options.
3. Analyze them and pick the best course of action for you.
4. Make a plan.
5. If you need assistance, choose it carefully.
6. Above all, remain flexible and don't be afraid to adjust your plan as you go along.

Good Luck!

Appendices

APPENDIX A

NUMISMATIC FRATERNAL ORGANIZATIONS

American Numismatic Association (ANA)
818 North Cascade Avenue
Colorado Springs, CO 80903
1-719-632-2646
FAX 1-719-634-4085
E-mail: ana@money.org
Web site: money.org

The American Numismatic Association is the country's largest collector organization for coins and related items. Formed in 1891, the ANA offers educational programs, an authentication service (no grading), and a monthly magazine, *Numismatist*. Its Colorado Springs headquarters features a first-rate museum and library that are available to members and non-members alike. The ANA offers renowned summer seminars on a number of numismatic subjects and holds two conventions annually. These shows offer 250 to 500 bourse tables and significant auctions. The annual convention auction (held in July or August) is frequently the best grossing auction sale of the year.

Professional Numismatists Guild (PNG)
3950 Concordia Lane
Fallbrook, CA 92028
1-760-728-1300
FAX 1-760-728-8507
E-mail: info@pngdealers.com
Web site: pngdealers.com

The Professional Numismatists Guild is the preeminent dealer group in the coin industry. Formed in 1955 with the motto, "Knowledge, Integrity, Responsibility," the PNG accepts members only after stringent background and financial investigations, and a vote of the entire membership. Members agree to uphold a strict code of ethics and to resolve any complaints against them through binding PNG arbitration. Lists of PNG dealers are available from the organization.

American Numismatic Society (ANS)
140 William Street
New York, NY 10038
212-234-3130
FAX: 1-212-234-3381
E-mail: info@amnumsoc.org
Web site: amnumsoc.org

The American Numismatic Society was founded in 1858, and is dedicated to the serious study of numismatic items. To that end, they have an extensive research library and world-class collections, and provide members and visiting scholars with a broad selection of publications, topical meetings and symposia, fellowships and grants, honors and awards, and various educational projects. Membership information can be obtained at their website or by telephone. The ANS hopes to be moved into their new location during 2004, so call for latest information regarding location and visiting hours.

APPENDIX B

INSURANCE COMPANIES OFFERING COLLECTIBLE & NUMISMATIC COVERAGE

Cleland & Associates
P O Box 899
Galveston, TX 77553-0899
1-409-766-7101
FAX: 1-409-766-7102
Contact: Richard Cleland

North American Collectibles Association
2316 Carrollton Road
Westminster, MD 21157
1-800-685-6746
1-410-857-5011
FAX 1-410-857-5259
Contact: Barbara Wingo
E-mail: nacabdw@aol.com

Woller, Seabury & Smith
1440 N. Northwest Highway
Park Ridge, IL 60068-1400
1-800-323-2106
1-847-803-3100

Hugh Wood, Inc.
(American Agent for Lloyds of London)
45 Broadway, 3rd Floor
New York, NY 10006
1-212-509-3777
FAX: 1-212-509-4906
Contact: Jack Fisher

APPENDIX C

THIRD-PARTY GRADING SERVICES

BASEBALL CARDS

Sportscard Guaranty LLC
P.O. Box 6919
Parsippany, NJ 07054-6919
1-800-SGC-9212
1-973-984-0018
FAX: 1-973-984-8447

PSA, Professional Sports Authenticator
P.O. Box 6180 Newport Beach, CA 92658
1-800-325-1121,
1-949-833-8824
FAX: 1-949-833-7955
Email: info@psacard.com

Beckett Grading Services (BGS)
Website: beckett.com/grading

COINS

Numismatic Guaranty Corporation of America (NGC)
P.O. Box 4776
Sarasota, FL 34230
1-800-NGC-COIN toll free
941-360-3990
FAX: 941-360-2553

A N A C S
P O Box 182141
Columbus, OH 43218
1-800-888-1861
FAX: 1-614-791-9103
Web Site: anacs.com

Professional Coin Grading Service (PCGS)
P O Box 9458
Newport Beach, CA 92658
1-800-447-8848
1-949-833-0600
FAX: 1-949-833-7660

COINS NEEDING CLEANING OR CONSERVATION

Numismatic Conservation Services (NCS)
P.O. Box 4750
Sarasota, FL 34230
1-866-627-2646
1-941-360-3996
ncscoin.com

COMICS

Comics Guaranty, LLC
P.O. Box 4738
Sarasota, FL 34230
1-877-NM-COMIC (toll free)
1-941-360-3991
FAX: 941-360-2558

APPENDIX D

SELECTED PUBLICATIONS FOR COLLECTORS

ARTWORK & PAPER COLLECTIBLES

How to Care for Works of Art on Paper
by Francis W. Dolloff, Roy L. Perkinson

Conservation Concerns: A Guide for Collectors and Curators
by Konstanze Bachmann, Dianne Pilgrim

Caring for Your Art
by Jill Snyder, Joseph Montague, Maria Reidelbach

BASEBALL CARDS

The Official Price Guide to Baseball Cards
by James Beckett

BOOKS & MANUSCRIPTS

Antiquarian Booksellers Association of American (ABAA.org) posts links to member published books and articles on collecting Rare Books and Manuscripts

How to Identify and Collect American First Editions
Arco Publishing, New York (1976) – (No longer in print—ironically, you will probably have to find a rare copy)

We also recommend: **ABEBooks.com** as a source of books on the Internet

COINS

The New York Times Guide to Coin Collecting: Do's, Don'ts, Facts, Myths, and a Wealth of History
by Ed Reiter

How to Grade U.S. Coins
by James L. Halperin

A Guide Book of United States Coins
by R. S. Yeoman

The Standard Catalog of World Coins
by Chester Krause & Clifford Mishler

COMICS

The Official Overstreet Comic Book Price Guide (Overstreet Comic Book Price Guide)
by Robert M. Overstreet – available digitally at HeritageComics.com

FURNITURE

The Bulfinch Anatomy of Antique Furniture: An Illustrated Guide to Identifying Period, Detail, and Design
by Tim Forrest, Paul Atterbury

American Antique Furniture: A Book for Amateurs, Vol. 1
by Jr. Edgar G. Miller

Miller's Collecting Furniture: Facts at Your Fingertips
by Christopher Payne

GUNS

The Gun Digest Book of Modern Gun Values: For Modern Arms Made from 1900 to Present (Gun Digest Book of Modern Gun Values, 11th Ed)
by Ken Ramage

Antique Guns: The Collector's Guide
by John E. Traister

1998 Standard Catalog of Firearms: The Collector's Price & Reference Guide (8th Ed)
by Ned Schwing

JEWELRY

Signed Beauties of Costume Jewelry: Identification & Values
by Marcia Sparkles Brown

Vintage Jewelry: A Price and Identification Guide, 1920 to 1940s
by Leigh Leshner

Antique Trader Jewelry Price Guide
by Kyle Husfloen, Marion Cohen

PAINTINGS AND SCULPTURE

AskART.com
United States artists only

ArtNet.com
International artists

TOYS

Official Hake's Price Guide to Character Toys
By Ted Hake

Cartoon Toys & Collectibles Identification and Value Guide
by David Longest

ALL COLLECTIBLES AND FINE ARTS

Maloney's Antiques & Collectibles Resource Directory
By David J. Maloney, Jr.

For Additional Resources in all Collector categories, please visit our Resources list at:

HeritageGalleries.com

Where we will also invite you to take our Collector survey to qualify for free auction catalogs and a drawing to win valuable prizes.

APPENDIX E

HERITAGEGALLERIES.COM RESOURCES

HeritageGalleries.com™ is a comprehensive corporate website that represents all of our expanding areas of interest. It provides information about all of our auction sites, which currently include:
- HeritageCoins.com
- HeritageCurrency.com
- HeritageComics.com
- HeritageMoviePosters.com
- HeritageSportsCollectibles.com
- HeritageAutographs.com

Coming soon:
- HeritageRareBooks.com
- HeritageFineArts.com
- HeritageRareJewelry.com

When visiting HeritageGalleries.com, you will be able to easily move from one collectible site to another.

James L. Halperin, professional rare coin dealer, futurist and best-selling science fiction novelist, as well as co-owner of Heritage Galleries, shares some of his insights about collecting in "The Intelligent Collector" section of HeritageGalleries.com.

What is your passion? Tell us what you collect for a chance to win a prize by taking our confidential survey at HeritageGalleries.com

Also on **HeritageGalleries.com**:
- Dates for our online and onsite auctions.
- Consigning to Heritage—learn how we can get the most for your collectibles.
- Trust and estate services and appraisals.

MyCollection™ is a free, private record of coins that you own, buy, or sell. It is designed to help you track information about—and current market value of—your collection. MyCollection allows you to actually store records on-line for easy reference, real-time valuations, and printouts for insurance or estate purposes.

Features

1. You will instantly know the current market value of your coins.
2. You can use a bar code scanner for NGC and PCGS certified coins for quick data entry into your collection.
3. You can see the auction prices realized history of each coin in your collection with one click.
4. You can subdivide your collection into as many different collections as you want.
5. You can assign each coin within your collections to categories of your own choosing.
6. MyCollection provides this privacy assurance: Your information will not be shared with, or sold to, any third party for any reason.
7. If you have purchased coins from Heritage, all of your coins will appear automatically in a "collection" called "Coins from Heritage." No need to enter those coins—we will do it for you!
8. Demand Rating. A demand rating is displayed for each coin in your collection. The ratings are derived from our MyWantlist™ data, and tell you how many HeritageCoin.com clients are actively looking for any given coin.

9. Sell Now Option. Each coin has a Sell Now option that you can use to quickly and effortlessly alert Heritage when you are considering selling a particular coin.

MyCollection is easy to use, but best of all—you are in control. You choose how to organize your collection.

http://www.heritagecoin.com/myheritage/mycollection/mycollectionlist.asp

My WantList™ is designed to find the items you are looking for from our extensive inventory and auction offerings. By taking just a few moments to enter the types and grading criteria of the items you want, our system will instantly search and display all matches.

After you opt in to My Wantlist™, Heritage will alert you periodically via email to new inventory and auction selections. You are never under any obligation and you may withdraw or update your Want List at any time. If you have any questions, please do not hesitate to contact us.

Just 3 Easy Steps

1. Click on any My WantList™ link:
   On any Heritage specialty website (you can find them all listed at HeritageGalleries.com), you can get to your personal Want List. You will be required to login, or sign-up for free if you are not already a member.
2. Begin building your Want List:
   Start by selecting the type of item you want to add. Select from the list of available types by clicking on the drop-down list that reads "All." Scroll through the list and click the type you are interested in.
3. Choose a specific item or group of items:
   You can choose to add an entire category of items by selecting that option in the top section. Select a service and grade preference if desired. Click the "Add new item" button.

You can also select any individual item from the list in the bottom "My Want List" section. Once again, choose your preferred grading service and item grade if appropriate. Then click "Save Changes."

Features

1. Easy Want List setup process.
2. Instantly and constantly searches our extensive inventory and auction offering for your preferred items.
3. Searches are by types, dates, and grading criteria you select.
4. You receive automatic e-mails when an item you are looking for becomes available.
5. No Obligation. Having an on-line Want List is for your convenience and does not obligate you in any way. You may withdraw or update your list at any time.
6. Total Privacy. Your information will not be shared with any third party for any reason.
7. Want List notifications include links directly back to full-color images, pricing and population data, and results from previous auctions.

Happy hunting! E-mail us at **shop@HeritageCoins.com** if you have any questions.

Go to **HeritageGalleries.com** then find the specialized site you are looking for, and start by searching for items you collect. Even if nothing is available that day, you can opt in to My WantList™ for future notification whenever those items appear in our inventory or auctions.

ABOUT THE AUTHORS

James L. Halperin is Heritage's co-founder, and "may be the greatest coin mind of all time," according to David Hall, founder and CEO of the Professional Coin Grading Service (PCGS). Halperin's 1986 book, "How to Grade U.S. Coins," set the core standards for the major coin grading services. Earlier, he designed the first mainframe computer system used in numismatics, in 1975, which quickly catapulted his fledgling coin company to the top of the industry. In 1983, he merged businesses with Steve Ivy to form Heritage. A surprising percentage of the successful coin dealers in America have learned their craft working under Jim at one time or another. A life member and former Governor of the American Numismatic Association, Jim is also a member of the Professional Numismatists Guild.

In 2001, Jim spearheaded Heritage's auction foray into comic books and popular culture, the success of which encouraged Heritage's expansion into numerous other categories of collectibles.

Since marrying in 1984, Jim and his wife Gayle have collected early 20th century American paintings (especially Maxfield Parrish), sculpture (especially Harriett Frishmuth), posters (especially Mucha) and art glass, EC and MAD comic books, comic art (especially EC artists, plus Robert Crumb, Frank Frazetta and Simon Bisley), 1960s fanzines, movie lobby cards, American and colonial currency, numismatic medals, among other tangents. He is now designing a web site to display the collection online. Jim also wrote two internationally best-selling science fiction novels in 1995 and 1996, then used all the royalties to endow a multi-million-dollar health education foundation.

Gregory J. Rohan is the President of Heritage with direct responsibility for all corporate functions involving rare coins. A numismatic prodigy who ran a successful rare coin business while still in high school, Greg has bought and sold millions of dollars in rare coins, including many famous rarities such as the 1804 silver dollar. He was instrumental in Heritage's Guinness World Record purchase of the Trompeter Collection for $15,177,000. With over three decades in the numismatic industry, Greg is intimately familiar with the handling of rare coins in estates and trusts, particularly where timing and taxation is an issue. He holds memberships in the Professional Numismatists Guild, the American Numismatic Association, YPO, and many other numismatic and professional organizations.

In 2003, he was appointed to a three-year term on the Small Business Advisory Board at the Federal Reserve Bank of Dallas. Greg and his wife Lysa have collected early 20th century silver, American Indian textiles, movie posters, rare wine, and contemporary glass by Dale Chihuly.

James L. Halperin

Gregory J. Rohan